MEDĪNET HABU.
View of pylon and chapel of Nektanebos.

LUXOR &
ITS TEMPLES
BY A·M·BLACKMAN D.LITT
ILLUSTRATED BY
MAJOR·BENTON
FLETCHER·

ISBN: 978-1-63923-917-7

All Rights reserved. No part of this book maybe reproduced without written permission from the publishers, except by a reviewer who may quote brief passages in a review to be printed in a newspaper or magazine.

Printed: March 2023

Published and Distributed By:
Lushena Books
607 Country Club Drive, Unit E
Bensenville, IL 60106
www.lushenabks.com

ISBN: 978-1-63923-917-7

PREFACE

IT was as long ago as December, 1913, when Major Fletcher was staying with me in my camp at Meir, in Asyūt province, that he and I first discussed the possibility of bringing out together a popularly written account of life as led by the inhabitants of ancient Thebes, I supplying the text and he the illustrations.

Upon the outbreak of the Great War any idea we entertained of such an undertaking was inevitably given up. However, the interest aroused by the late Lord Carnarvon and Mr. Howard Carter's discovery in the Valley of the Tombs of the Kings brought the old project back to our minds; and when Major Fletcher was approached by Messrs. A. and C. Black on the subject of producing a book about Luxor, to which he was to supply the illustrations, he at once wrote to me asking me to do what I had often talked about doing with him in the past. Hence this book, which it is hoped will convince its readers that Egyptology is not a dreary study, but is full of human interest—is, in fact, concerned rather with life and beauty than with mummies and other dusty trophies of death.

To Professor Sir W. M. Flinders Petrie and other friends I tender my sincere thanks for kindly permitting me to use illustrations from their published works.

In conclusion, let me say that it will give me no little satisfaction if this small volume, so admirably illustrated by Major Fletcher's pencil drawings, succeeds, as it is intended to do, in increasing the interest of the general public in Ancient Egypt, and so, incidentally, in adding to the list of subscribers to the Egypt Exploration Society, under the auspices of which a great part of my research work in Egypt has been conducted.

AYLWARD M. BLACKMAN.

CONTENTS

	PAGE
TABLE OF DATES	x

CHAPTER I
LIFE IN ANCIENT LUXOR

CHAPTER II
HOW THEBES BECAME THE CAPITAL OF EGYPT — 35

CHAPTER III
THEBES, THE WORLD'S FIRST MONUMENTAL CITY — 58

CHAPTER IV
SOME GREAT KINGS IN TIME OF WAR — 84

CHAPTER V
A FAMOUS QUEEN — 111

CHAPTER VI
POEMS, SONGS, AND ROMANCES — 136

CHAPTER VII
SOME FUNERARY TEMPLES — 160

BIBLIOGRAPHY — 191

INDEX — 195

LIST OF FULL-PAGE PLATES

FROM DRAWINGS BY
MAJOR BENTON FLETCHER

PLATE

I. Medīnet Habu	-	*Frontispiece*
		FACING PAGE
II. Luxor Ferry -	-	1
III. Floral Columns, Karnak -		8
IV. Great Hypostyle Hall, Karnak -	·	17
V. Great Hypostyle Hall, Karnak -	·	24
VI. Temple of Khons, Karnak -		33
VII. Sacred Lake, Karnak - -		40
VIII. Colonnaded Court, Temple of Luxor		49
IX. Hypostyle Hall, Temple of Luxor		56
X. Nefretiri - - - -		65
XI. Head of a Young Man -		72
XII. Native School -		81
XIII. The Nile at Luxor -		88
XIV. Wife of Ramesses II.	-	97
XV. Deir El-Baḥri -	-	104
XVI. Deir El-Baḥri -	-	113

LIST OF FULL-PAGE PLATES

PLATE		FACING PAGE
XVII.	RAMESSEUM	120
XVIII.	RAMESSEUM	129
XIX.	HYPOSTYLE HALL, RAMESSEUM	136
XX.	RAMESSEUM	140
XXI.	MEDÎNET HABU	145
XXII.	HIGH GATE OF RAMESSES III.	152
XXIII.	COLOSSAL STATUE, THEBES	161
XXIV.	TOMBS OF THE KINGS	168

Sketch-Map of the District on p. xii

There are also fifty line illustrations inserted throughout the text.

TABLE OF DATES*

THE OLD KINGDOM
2900-2475 B.C.
Fourth Dynasty, 2900-2750 B.C.
Fifth Dynasty, 2750-2625 B.C.
Sixth Dynasty, 2625-2475 B.C.

FIRST INTERMEDIATE PERIOD
INCLUDING THE
Seventh and Eighth Dynasties, 2475-2445 B.C.
Ninth and Tenth Dynasties, 2445-2160 B.C.

THE MIDDLE KINGDOM
2160-1788 B.C.
Eleventh Dynasty, 2160-2000 B.C.
Twelfth Dynasty, 2000-1788 B.C.

AMENEMḤĒT I.	- 2000-1970 B.C.	{ 2000-1980 B.C., alone. 1980-1970 B.C., with his son.
SESŌSTRIS I.	- 1980-1935 B.C.	{ 1980-1970 B.C., with his father. 1970-1938 B.C., alone. 1938-1935 B.C., with his son.
AMENEMḤĒT II.	- 1938-1903 B.C.	{ 1938-1935 B.C., with his father. 1935-1906 B.C., alone. 1906-1903 B.C., with his son.
SESŌSTRIS II.	- 1906-1887 B.C.	{ 1906-1903 B.C., with his father. 1903-1887 B.C., alone.
SESŌSTRIS III.	- 1887-1849 B.C.	Uncertain period with his son.
AMENEMḤĒT III.	- 1849-1801 B.C.	{ Uncertain period with his father. Uncertain period with his son.
AMENEMḤĒT IV.	- 1801-1792 B.C.	Uncertain period with his father.
SEBKNEFRURĒʿ	- 1792-1788 B.C.	

---

* In accordance with Breasted, " A History of Egypt." London, 1906, pp. 597 *foll.*

TABLE OF DATES

THE SECOND INTERMEDIATE PERIOD
1788 – 1580 B.C.

INCLUDING THE

Thirteenth to Seventeenth Dynasties and the Hyksōs,
1788–1580 B.C.

THE NEW KINGDOM, OR IMPERIAL AGE,
1580–1167 B.C.

Eighteenth Dynasty, 1580–1350 B.C.

AḤMŌSE I.	1580–1557 B.C.
AMENḤOTPE I.	1557–1536 B.C.
DḤUTMŌSE I. }	
DḤUTMŌSE II. }	
ḤATSHEPSUT }	1536–1447 B.C.
DḤUTMŌSE III. }	
AMENḤOTPE II.	1447–1420 B.C.
DḤUTMŌSE IV.	1420–1411 B.C.
AMENḤOTPE III.	1411–1375 B.C.
AKHENATON }	
SAKERĒ' }	1375–1350 B.C.
TUT'ENKHAMŪN }	
AY }	

Nineteenth Dynasty, 1350–1205 B.C.

ḤAREMḤEB	1350–1315 B.C.
RAMESSES I.	1315-1314 B.C.
SETI I.	1313–1292 B.C.
RAMESSES II.	1292–1225 B.C.
MERNEPTAḤ	1225–1215 B.C.
AMENMESES	1215 B.C.
SIPTAḤ	1215–1209 B.C.
SETI II.	1209–1205 B.C.

Interim of Anarchy, 1205–1200 B.C.

Twentieth Dynasty, 1200–1090 B.C.

SETNAKHT	1200–1198 B.C.
RAMESSES III.	1198–1167 B.C.
RAMESSES IV.–RAMESSES XII.	1167–1090 B.C.

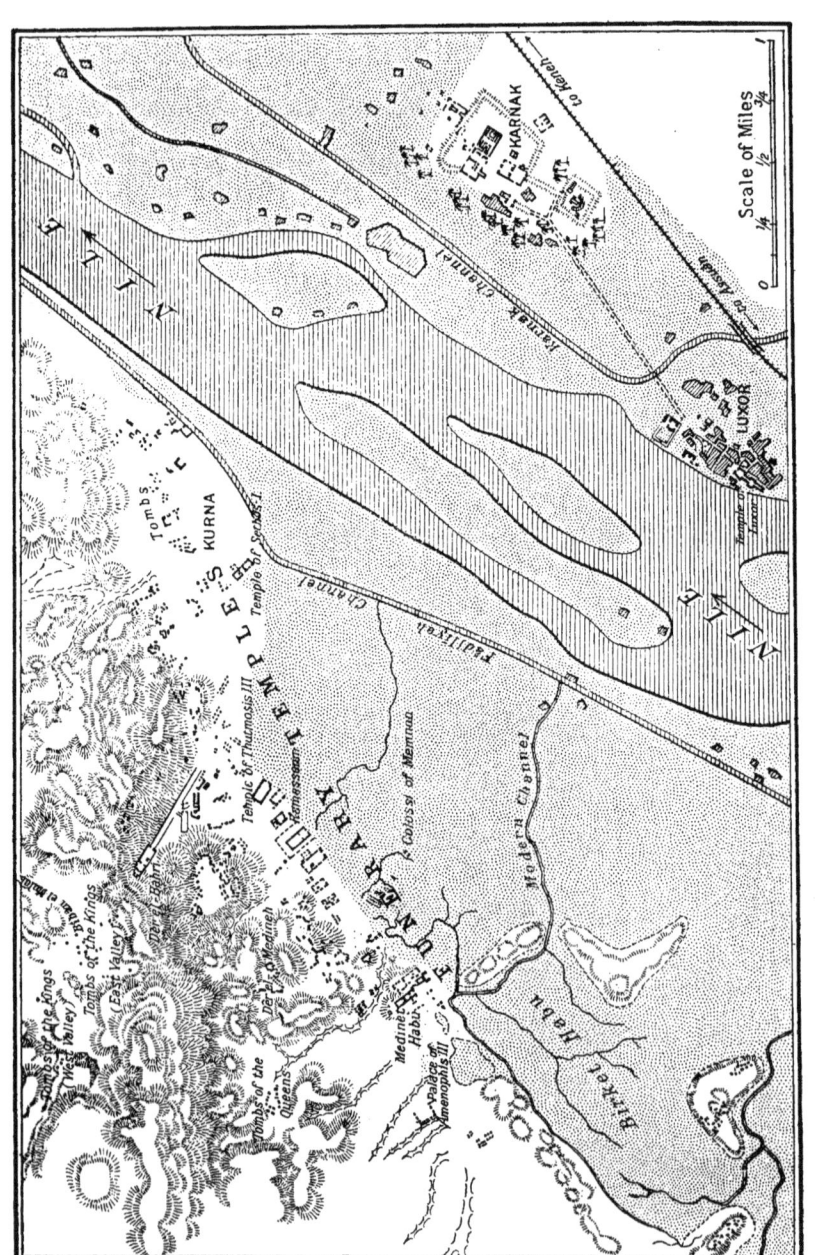

LUXOR FERRY.
View from left bank of Nile towards the Temple of Luxor. (See pp. 83, 184.)

LUXOR AND ITS TEMPLES

CHAPTER I

LIFE IN ANCIENT LUXOR

THE first question that anybody would ask who wanted to know something of the life led by the ancient inhabitants of Luxor—or Thebes as it was called by the Greek and Latin writers—would in all probability be : " What sort of houses did they live in ?" So I propose to begin the first chapter of this book by giving as briefly as possible what will, I hope, be a satisfactory answer to this by no means unintelligent question.

Excavations have shown us that an Egyptian town presented much the same appearance in ancient as in modern times. There were the same narrow streets and the same sort of houses, the latter constructed of mud-brick, sometimes white-washed or colour-washed, and consisting, in the case of well-to-do folk, of a ground floor and one or two upper stories. A painting in the tomb chapel of a certain Theban royal scribe named Dhutnūfer, who flourished some time about the year 1450 B.C., depicts just such a two-storied house, that of the royal scribe himself (see Fig. 1). It will be seen that flights of stairs lead from one floor to another and on to the flat roof, where, as at the present day, are placed domed granaries made of mud. No doubt, then as now, alongside of the granaries was stacked the household fuel— bundles of brushwood and maize-stalks and cakes of cow-dung. The roof in ancient, no less than in modern, Egypt was the women's favourite resort, the place where they not only gathered to gossip and enjoy the air, but also to do a great deal of their work, spinning, sewing, and even cooking.

The ground floor of Dhutnūfer's house, it will be seen, is given up to the kitchen, and also to workrooms, where men and women are engaged in spinning and weaving. These workpeople are either members of Dhutnūfer's household, or else that individual let out the greater part of the ground floor of his house to a weaver, who used the rooms as his business premises.

On the first floor were Dhutnūfer's own apartments, where he also received his friends. The women's quarters, as in a modern Egyptian house, occupied the top floor. It will be noted that the actual rooms shown by the artist are of fine dimensions, the ceilings being supported on columns, doubtless made of wood.

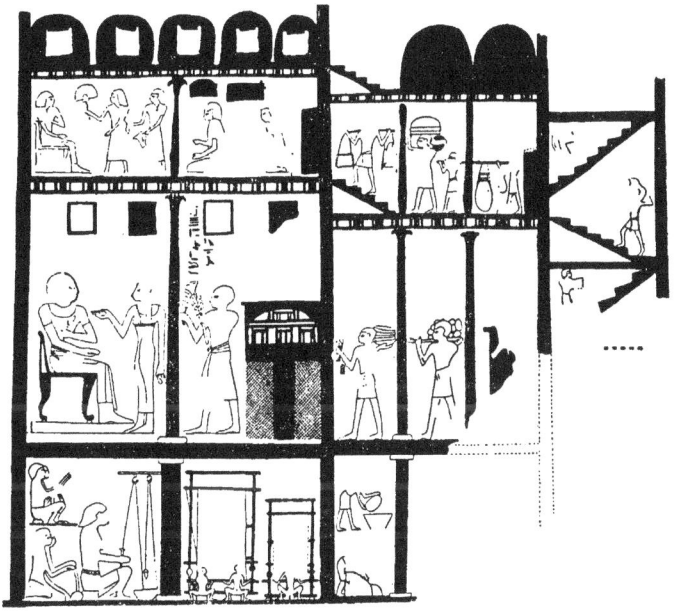

Fig. 1.—Dhutnūfer's House.
(*After* "*Ancient Egypt,*" *iii. By the courtesy of Professor Sir W. M. Flinders Petrie.*)

In respect of its furnishing and decoration, such a house as that of Dhutnūfer would, though less magnificent, have been very much like one of the larger mansions now to be described.

The excavations of the Egypt Exploration Society

and the Deutsche Orient - Gesellschaft at El-Amarna have laid bare the remains of some once splendid houses, doubtless similar to those that belonged to the great nobles and officials of ancient Luxor, and resembling in many respects the dwellings of the great pashas and beys of to-day. Such houses stood each in the midst of an enclosure, often covering a large area, surrounded by high, sometimes crenellated, walls of crude brick (see Fig. 4). To this enclosure admittance was gained from the street by an imposing gateway, outside which, on a couple of low brick benches, sat a small group of servants, whose business it was to supervise the ingress and egress of members of the household and of clients, and to attend to the wants of visitors. Such a group of servants is regularly to be seen sitting beside the entrance to a pasha's residence in modern Cairo.

In one corner of the enclosure were the great man's stables, cowsheds, storehouses, and granaries —for wealth in those days consisted not in money but in produce—and close to them the quarters of the male servants. In an entirely different part of the grounds was the residence of the wife's female attendants and those ladies who found favour with the master of the house, but did not hold the privileged status of wife. It was to such ladies, no doubt, who, however, occupied a recognized position in the household, that the euphemistic title of " sisters " was assigned.

The actual mansion—a ground plan of a typical El-Amarna house appears as Fig. 2—stood in the

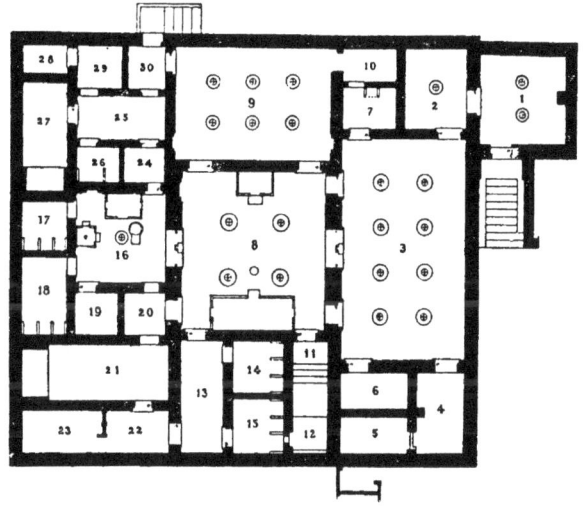

Fig. 2.—Ground Plan of a Mansion at El-Amarna.

(*After* " *Journal of Egyptian Archæology,*" *viii. By the courtesy of Professor Peet and Messrs. C. L. Woolley and Newton.*)

middle of the enclosure, and a flight of shallow steps led up to the front door. On the ground floor were a number of fine rooms, the ceilings, painted bright blue, resting upon wooden columns, which were also painted in gay colours. The walls of these apartments were white, except for a painted frieze, which generally took the form of floral garlands or festoons, a bunch of dead waterfowl being occasionally represented hanging head downwards between each pair of festoons, a foretaste of the still-life pictures of the seventeenth century Dutch painters! Sometimes, too, the wall-space of these rooms was broken by a painted recess, or a couple of such recesses, resembling somewhat the *ḳibleh* in a mosque, and perhaps serving a religious as well as a decorative purpose.

Of the pillared apartments, one generally lay on the north side of the house (Room 3 of the plan) and one on the west side (Room 9), the northern room being a favourite resort in summer and the western in winter. These two rooms had large windows down one wall—the outside wall of the house in either case—filled with stone gratings, which broke up the strong light in an agreeable manner.

Between these two apartments, the north and west galleries, as they might well be called, lay two other pillared rooms, evidently reception or dining rooms, the one (Room 8) probably intended for the entertainment of guests (see Fig. 3), and the other (Room 16) reserved for the use of the family. In either dining-room there was a dais, on

LIFE IN ANCIENT LUXOR 7

which possibly were placed chairs for the master of the house and for the principal persons among those who partook of a meal in his company. There was also a stone platform, built against one of the walls, with a stone screen at the back, and

Fig. 3.—A Pillared Reception Room.
(*After " Journal of Egyptian Archæology," viii. By the courtesy of Professor Peet and Messrs. C. L. Woolley and Newton.*)

on this people performed their ablutions, for the ancient Egyptians indulged in a great deal of rather elaborate washing both before meals and at other times. A hollow was cut in the platform to receive the large jar which contained the ablution water. The jar is shown in the adjacent cut (Fig. 3) standing in position.

These two dining-rooms were lit by grated windows set high up in the walls, and their ceilings rose well above the roof of the upper-story rooms, which did not extend above these two apartments. In the dining-room used for guests were a number of doors, including two fine folding doors, admitting to the two pillared galleries, the private dining-room and other rooms, and also to the staircase leading to the upper floor.

In either dining-room there was a receptacle in the floor for the portable hearth or brazier, which, as in the modern Egyptian house, was used in the cold weather, the fuel employed being charcoal.

The rest of the ground floor was taken up by two bedrooms (Rooms 21 and 27)—the bed standing on a low dais in a recess—and a number of smaller rooms. These and the bedrooms had no windows, and light could only have been admitted through the doors and through gratings above the doors. But whatever light managed to get in was intensified by the whitewashed walls. It should be noted that either bedroom had a bathroom and lavatory attached to it (Rooms 22, 23, and 28, 29).

Some of the smaller rooms (Nos. 14, 15, 17, and

18) were certainly store-rooms, being furnished with broad shelves placed on brick supports. The rest may have been used as sleeping apartments by less important members of the household, relatives and confidential servants. The kitchen was a separate building all to itself.

There was at least one upper story, which was probably given up entirely, or in the main, to the women. Certain of the upper rooms were pillared like those downstairs.

Such a house was beautifully though simply furnished. The floors of the principal rooms, which were of unburnt brick or tiles, appear to have been covered with matting, on which brightly coloured rugs or carpets were also sometimes laid. Occasionally such covering was dispensed with and the floor was painted, though never, so it would seem, with the beautiful designs, described in Chapter III., which were employed for the decoration of the floors of the royal palaces.

The more important rooms no doubt contained a number of chairs and stools, the best of these being made of ebony, or other precious woods, inlaid with ivory; or else the wood was overlaid with gold and sometimes inlaid as well with richly coloured glaze plaques. The chairs and stools often had seats woven out of palm-leaves, looking exactly like the cane seats of our modern chairs, and on these were laid cushions covered with leather or some woven material.

People reposed at night on couches, the legs of which, as also the legs of the chairs, were carved in semblance of those of a lion.

Other articles of furniture were boxes and caskets, often elaborately carved, gilded, and inlaid, in which were kept clothing and jewelry.

A large portion of the enclosure surrounding a great house was laid out as a formal garden (see Fig. 4). Part of such a garden was often, as in modern Egypt, given up to trellised vines, the remaining space being occupied by ornamental and fruit-bearing trees. There was also generally a pond in the garden, sometimes more than one, overshadowed by clumps of papyrus and other swamp-loving plants and bushes. In the pond itself grew lotus flowers, among which swam duck and other water-fowl, and also all manner of fish.

A love for nature animate and inanimate seems to have been a marked characteristic of the ancient Egyptians. A wealthy man gathered into his garden all the plants and flowers he could obtain; indeed, as we shall see in a subsequent chapter,

Fig. 4.—A House in its Surrounding Grounds.
(*After* Perrot *and* Chipiez, "*Histoire de l'Art dans a l'Antiquité.*")

certain of the Pharaohs brought strange trees, shrubs, and plants from abroad, and planted them in the gardens and parks attached to the royal palaces and the temples. Near the pond or ponds in the garden a gaily painted wooden pavilion was often erected, in which the master of the demesne could sit either alone or accompanied by wife and friends, and unobserved watch the antics of the water-fowl as they swam and dived among the water-lilies, preened their feathers on the bank, or sat in their nests amid the reeds. This love of the Egyptians for nature appears in the floral wall-decorations in their houses, but especially in the paintings and reliefs with which they adorned their tomb-chapels and the royal palaces.

It was not in his garden only that the Egyptian gentleman practised the cult of the open-air life. Among his favourite pastimes were fishing and fowling, and hunting the hippopotamus, in back-water, swamp, and river, and big-game shooting in the desert.

When fishing for sport the ancient Egyptian generally employed a double-bladed harpoon, and the artist, who represented his patron indulging in this form of amusement, always flatteringly shows him, as in Fig. 5, just in the act of hoisting his harpoon out of the water with a great fish transfixed on either blade! When wielding this formidable-looking weapon the noble or gentle harpooner stood in the middle of a boat made of papyrus reeds cunningly fastened together. He is always depicted accompanied by one or more male attendants, often a son or two as well, and nearly always

Fig. 5.—Egyptian Gentleman Fowling and Fishing.
(*After Wilkinson, " Manners and Customs of the Ancient Egyptians."*)

one or more of his ladies—his wife and a daughter or two. He used a similar boat and was similarly accompanied when he was fowling. Standing in the middle of the frail-looking craft (see Fig. 6), we see him hurling his throw-stick at the cloud of birds hovering above the dense papyrus thickets, which grow down to the water's edge.

Sometimes when out for a day's fowling the ancient sportsman took a cat with him, the animal having been trained to catch birds and bring them to its master (see Fig. 6). These fishing and fowl-

Fig. 6.—A Fowler hurling his Throw-Stick.
(*After Wilkinson.*)

ing scenes are very attractive. On the surface of the bright blue water float beautiful lotus flowers together with their flat circular green leaves, and in and out amid their stalks swim fishes great and small with wonderful iridescent scales. The papyrus thickets swarm with birds of all kinds, which wade in the shallows, or fly overhead, or sit on their eggs in their nests, or hover protectingly above their half-fledged young. Among the birds are to be seen butterflies and dragon-flies.

The ladies are dressed in their best clothes and wear brightly coloured ornaments. The wife is sometimes depicted standing beside her lord, often with her arm lovingly cast round his waist—surely a rather ill-timed display of affection! Often, too, she sits quietly in the bottom of the boat with the other ladies, and contents herself with embracing the marital ankle! The ladies generally hold bunches of lotus flowers, and they may also be seen carrying the birds that have been brought down by the well-aimed throw-stick. In a well-known Theban tomb-chapel picture a young girl is represented leaning over the side of the boat and plucking a blue and white lotus flower to add to the nosegays carried by the older female members of the party.

The ladies seem to have accompanied the men even when they engaged in the dangerous sport of hunting the hippopotamus. A painting in one of the Theban tomb-chapels (Fig. 7), now, unhappily, completely destroyed, shows us the royal herald,

Intef, standing up in one of the usual papyrus boats, and in the act of hurling his harpoon at one of these monsters. A rope, we learn, was attached to the blade, so that when the great beast had been trans-

Fig. 7.—Hunting the Hippopotamus.
(*After Wilkinson.*)

fixed the blade could still be controlled by the rope, which could be drawn in or let out as the situation demanded. In the picture in question the animal has already been pierced three times, and Intef

GREAT HYPOSTYLE HALL, KARNAK.
View down central aisle towards obelisk of Dhutmose I. (See pp. 60 foll.)

holds in his left hand the ropes attached to the three blades. An attendant is trying to cast a noose over the enraged monster's head.

When an ancient Egyptian gentleman went a-hunting in the desert he left all the members of the ḥarīm behind him, and was accompanied only by men. Permanent, or perhaps only temporary, enclosures were constructed in the desert, into which was gathered together game (or what the ancient Egyptians reckoned game) of every description (see Fig. 8)—oryxes, ibexes, gazelles, hyenas, ostriches, hares, and even hedgehogs! The hunter, who was either on foot or rode in a two-horse chariot is depicted by the ancient artist as shooting arrow after arrow into the miscellaneous herd of animals, who rush away from him in headlong flight. The hunter was accompanied by large and fierce hounds, which are regularly shown racing after the terrified creatures, and bringing down those that they have managed to catch up and spring upon.

The apartments of the wife and daughters and other chief female members of the family were, as has already been pointed out, upstairs. In the case of a large and wealthy establishment, the female attendants and the concubines, as also has been stated above, were lodged in a separate building.

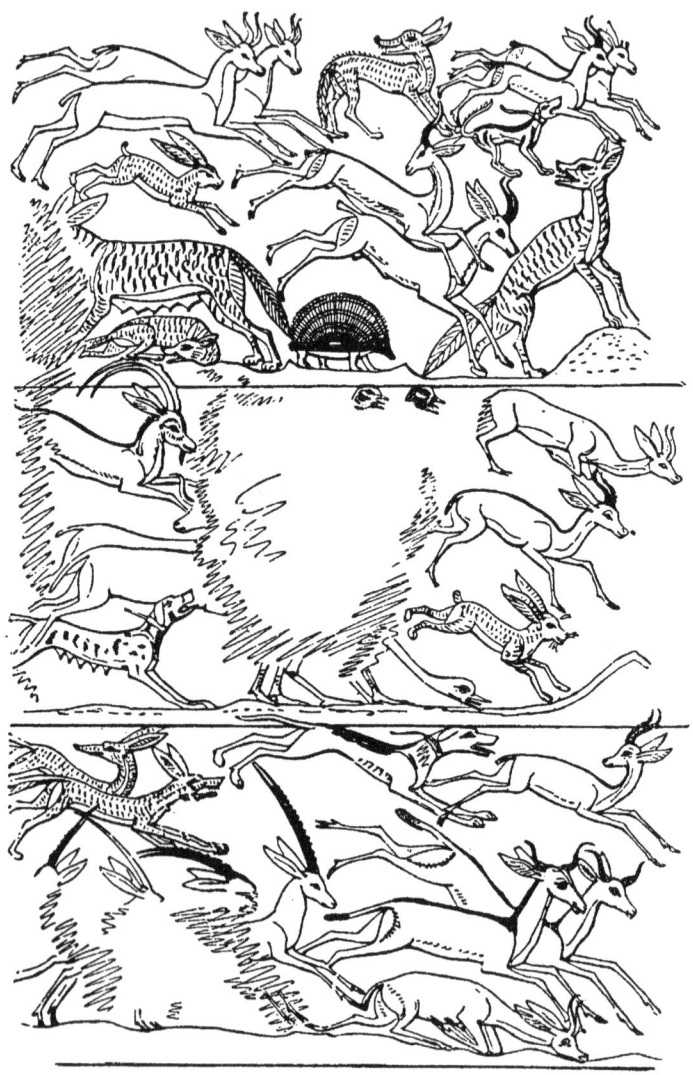

Fig. 8.—Part of a Theban Wall-Painting depicting a Desert Chase. (*After Wilkinson.*)

Here certain tomb-chapel reliefs depict them as entertaining one another with vocal and instrumental music and with dancing.

The women's quarters, especially in the house of a great noble or high official, where there would have been, particularly in the later Imperial Age, a number of concubines, were doubtless, as they are at the present day, hotbeds of intrigue. Indeed, fairly full details of a *ḥarīm* conspiracy, got up by the women of a very exalted household, the household of no less a person than the Emperor Ramesses III., are preserved to us in certain contemporary state documents.

One of Ramesses III.'s queens, we learn, plotted to make away with the king, who was now an old man and evidently in a bad state of health, her object being to place her own son on the throne. Various members of the royal household, some of them employed in the personal service of the Pharaoh, were implicated, chief among them being the Lord Chamberlain and a royal butler.

The Lord Chamberlain managed to acquire a number of wax figures of gods and men, and also some magical writings, all of which he succeeded in smuggling into the *ḥarīm*. By means of these, it was supposed, the palace guard could be bewitched and enfeebled, and thus the plot would not be discovered and foiled.

Wives of certain of the officers who kept guard over the gate of the ḥarīm were drawn into the plot, and were prevailed upon to convey messages to persons outside the palace precincts—namely, male relatives and friends of the ḥarīm inmates, who were urged to stir up the people of Luxor against the old Pharaoh. It is evident that what was aimed at was a revolution in the capital coinciding with the murderous *coup d'état* within the royal palace.

But, despite all precautions, information reached the ears of those who were still faithful to their lawful sovereign that a plot was brewing. Perhaps one of the conspirators thought better of it and turned king's evidence, for the authorities evidently were furnished with a long list of names, and all the persons known to be implicated in the conspiracy were arrested. A special tribunal was appointed to try the criminals, and those found guilty of the charges brought against them were executed or else allowed to commit suicide.

At this period of Egyptian history, the end of the Second Empire, the population of the capital was as mixed as that of modern Cairo, and many

LIFE IN ANCIENT LUXOR 21

of the highest positions about the Court were held by foreigners. Wealth, luxury, and the influx of foreigners from the conquered countries, had thoroughly corrupted the Egyptians of the upper classes, and it is not surprising to learn that even members of the special tribunal were susceptible to outside influence. The State documents, from which the account of the conspiracy and trials given above has been derived, inform us that two of the judges, after their appointment to the special tribunal, took part in a drinking bout with some of the accused women and one of their male confederates, and two officers who were responsible for the safe-keeping of the prisoners joined in the revels! The two judges and officers in question were brought to trial for this gross misconduct, and, being found guilty, were sentenced to have their noses and ears cut off. One of those thus mutilated, unable to bear the misery and disgrace inflicted on him, took his own life.

But this deals with the shady side of Egyptian domesticity. As a matter of fact, the ordinary husband and wife seem to have lived on the most affectionate terms with one another. Both in statuary and in reliefs and paintings the husband and wife are constantly depicted as sitting or standing side by side, she often with an arm thrown lovingly round his shoulders or waist. Husband, wife, and children all sat together at meat, and there was not that strict seclusion of women that is such a marked feature of modern Egyptian social life. As we shall see shortly, men and women sat side by side at banquets and other entertainments, and engaged one another in lively conversation. It has already been pointed out that ladies accompanied their husbands and male relations when they went fishing, fowling, and hippopotamus hunting.

What the relations of a man with his wife might be, even in the late Imperial Age, is revealed to us in a letter written by a widower to his dead spouse, the document being now preserved in the Museum at Leyden.

Some time after his wife's death the man fell sick and his medical adviser apparently informed him that she was annoyed with him for some reason or other, and was making him ill. The sick man, therefore, composed a letter *to the excellent ghost* of the dear departed, and having, doubtless, first read it aloud in the tomb-chapel on the occasion of one of the periodical celebrations therein of the funerary liturgy, fastened it to the wrathful lady's portrait-statue. By so doing, it was felt, the letter was bound to reach her.

What wrong have I done thee, he asks, *that I should be in this evil plight in which I now am? What have I done unto thee that thy hand should be set against me, seeing that I have done thee no wrong? From the time that I was with thee as husband until to-day, what have I done unto thee that I have had to conceal? I will stay in thy presence by means of the words of my mouth, in the presence of the nine gods of the West* (the gods of the world of the dead), *and one shall judge between thee and this letter which speaks with thee, namely this complaint. What have I done unto thee? Thou wast my wife when I was a stripling, and I was ever with thee. . . . When I exercised any office I was with thee. I never left thee nor made thy heart sorrowful. But see, thou dost not make my heart glad, therefore will I have the law of thee and one shall discern right from wrong.* He then points out to her how he magnified her in the eyes of his underlings. *Behold, when I was instructor of the officers of Pharaoh's host and chariotry, I made them come and bow themselves down before thee, and made them bring all good things to lay down in thy presence.* He again emphasizes the fact that he never had anything to conceal from her, insists that he was always a faithful husband, and boasts that in all his dealings with her he never gave cause for anyone to find fault with him. As the years went by and he was promoted, his duties kept him more and more in close attendance on the Pharaoh and prevented him from being continually in his wife's company—indeed, he was often compelled to be absent from home for considerable periods on end. But despite all that, *I sent thee my oil, my bread, and my clothing, and it was brought to thee. I did not send it elsewhere* (that is, to another woman). When he was away on duty with the Pharaoh his wife fell sick and died, but he insists that he never once failed to do all that an affectionate husband could do in the circumstances. *Behold*, he complains, *thou dost not know the good I have done thee. I sent to know how thou didst fare, and when thou was sick of the sickness that thou hadst, I sent thee a chief physician, and he prescribed and he did that which thou didst say should be done. When I accompanied Pharaoh on a journey to Upper Egypt, my thoughts were ever with thee, and I passed my stay of eight months without eating and drinking like a man. When I reached Memphis, I petitioned Pharaoh, and I betook me to*

GREAT HYPOSTYLE HALL, KARNAK.
View looking across the three aisles. (See pp. 60 foll.)

where thou art (where the wife lay dead), *and I bewailed thee exceedingly along with my household in front of my dwelling. I gave clothing of Upper Egyptian linen to wrap thee in, and I caused much clothing to be made for thee, leaving no good thing for thee undone. Now, behold, I have spent three years until now, remaining as I am and not entering into a house* (not getting married?), *though it is not becoming that one like me should be made to do so. . . . Behold, thou knowest not good from ill! But one shall decide between thee and me!* The end of the letter is rather amusing. The sick man thinks, perhaps owing to his previous knowledge of the lady, that cajolery will pay better with her than a threat of judgment to come. So he ends his letter as follows: *Behold the sisters in the house—I enter not in unto one of them!*

If love of husband and wife was a feature of family life in Ancient Egypt, still more so was the love of a son for his mother, a thing that is still most noticeable among the modern Egyptians, the mother always occupying the first place in her son's affections.

The following admonition addressed by the Sage Ani to his son Khenshotpe might be the words of any good Egyptian father of to-day: *Double the portion of bread that thou givest to thy mother, and support her as she once supported thee* (in her womb). *In thee she carried a heavy burden and she handed it not to me*—(i.e., I, your father, could not assist her in carrying thee). *When thou wast born after thine (appointed) months, she carried thee yet again about her neck, and for three years she suckled thee. . . . She placed thee at school when thou wast instructed in writing, and daily she waited there with bread and beer* (for thee) from her house. When thou art a young man and takest to thee a wife, and hast thine own household, keep before thee how thy mother hath borne thee and how she brought thee up in all manner of ways. May she not* (because of thy neglect) *bring evil upon thee by lifting up her hands to God, and he would hear her cry.*

This love for the mother did not exclude the mutual affection of father and son. As is quite evident from the inscriptions, it was the wish of every Egyptian father that his son should succeed him in his office—should *sit on his seat after he was gone*—and it was a son's duty to cause his father's name to live. In fact, piety to both parents was not to cease after death, and among the admonitions

* The staple food of the ancient Egyptians of both sexes and all ages and ranks.

of the sage Ani, from which a quotation has already been made, we find the following exhortation: *Offer water to thy father and thy mother who rest in the Western Valley* (the Theban necropolis). *Leave not that undone, so that thy son may do the like for thee.*

The custom of pouring out a libation of water at the graveside still survives in Upper Egypt and Lower Nubia, and is regularly practised on Friday, the Muhammadan Sabbath.

How deeply an Egyptian son could love his father comes out very clearly in an inscription which is to be found in the tomb-chapel of a certain noble, who flourished during the latter part of the Sixth Dynasty, about 2500 B.C. Though the inscription was composed a thousand years before the period with which this book deals, yet the passage in question so admirably illustrates the point raised that I shall hardly do amiss in quoting it: *I caused myself to be buried in one tomb with this Dau* (the father of the speaker), *in order that I might be with him in one place; not, however, through lack of means for making two tombs; but I did this in order that I might see this Dau daily, in order that I might be with him in one place.*

It is the aim of the writer of this book to eradicate from the minds of the general public the quite erroneous idea that the Ancient Egyptians were a gloomy people, people who were always brooding over death and preparing for the day of burial. On the contrary, they were a most cheerful and pleasure-loving folk, as are most of the dwellers in the sunny Mediterranean lands. As we shall see, they loved a good song, a good story, and were much addicted to the drinking of wine and beer. Among them were men of resource and courage, as well as artists, poets and religious thinkers. The pillared halls and reception-rooms of the wealthy must have been constantly furnished with hilarious guests, for, like their modern descendants, the ancient inhabitants of the Nile Valley were much given to hospitality, and thoroughly enjoyed entertaining and being entertained.

Thanks to the numerous paintings in the tomb-chapels, it is no very difficult matter to reconstruct a Theban banquet, which would have taken place in one of the pillared rooms—either the north or west gallery, or the dining-room. The men and women sat side by side on cushioned chairs, among the former being included members of the clergy, who are to be recognized by their shaven heads

LIFE IN ANCIENT LUXOR 29

(see Fig. 9). Before they began to eat and drink, the guests, each in turn, extended their hands over a basin held by one attendant, while another poured water over them from a ewer. Having wiped their hands on the napkin with which they were each

Fig. 9.—A Theban Dinner-Party.
(*After Wilkinson.*)

provided, they were fumigated with incense and their heads were anointed with liquid scent or else with a lump of perfumed grease. As the incense-laden air of the crowded reception-room became warmer and warmer, and the feasters got more and more heated with eating and drinking, the grease melted and ran down over their clothes and emitted what was considered to be a pleasant perfume. Often in pictures of banquets the upper portions of the guests' white linen clothes are represented as covered all over with yellow streaks, to indicate where the liquefied grease has trickled down from their brows! The female guests are nearly always depicted as crowned with a garland of lotus petals and as having inserted a bud or full-blown flower in the curls of their wigs just above the forehead, for in ancient Luxor great wigs, like those in vogue among our ancestors in the days of Charles II. and William and Mary, were worn by both sexes. The pictures also represent most of the guests as holding a lotus flower in one hand and occasionally as presenting it, or else a choice fruit, to a fellow guest to smell or taste respectively. The lotus flower seems to have played somewhat the same part at an ancient, as the cigarette does at a modern, Egyptian entertainment.

If the banquet took place after sunset, the room would have been illuminated by means of oil lamps placed on tall pottery stands. These lamps were shallow cups or saucers furnished with one or more floating wicks, the luminant being crude castor oil with salt put in it to keep the flame from smoking. As Mr. F. Ll. Griffith's recent experiments in

Oxford have shown, a very strong and steady white light is given by a floating-wick lamp supplied with crude castor oil, provided the salt is not omitted.

Numbers of small tables loaded with food of all kinds were placed beside the feasters, whose mode of eating was not entirely in accordance with our ideas of refinement. A great lady would take possession of a whole duck, and holding it in one hand would tear pieces off it with the other, or she might be seen gnawing at a whole leg or shoulder of mutton!

Great wine- and beer-jars stood in wooden racks, jars and racks being begarlanded with flowers and trailers of vine. As the banqueters ate and drank, minstrels played on pipes, lutes, and harps, and vocalists sang to the accompaniment of the music, rhythmically clapping their hands together as do the Egyptian singers of to-day. While the musicians played and sang, dancing-girls, clad in little else than jewelry, performed all manner of antics, waving their arms, and twisting and twirling their bodies now this way, now that. The servants kept plying the guests with wine and yet more wine, which was drunk out of gold, silver, or beautiful porcelain goblets. In one tomb-chapel of the early Imperial Age at El-Kāb the words written above a lady's head represent her as saying : *Give me eighteen cups of wine. Behold I should love (to drink) to drunkenness. My inside is as dry as straw!* In a Theban painting (see Fig. 10) a lady is depicted as being on the verge of collapsing altogether under the influence of the merry wine-god, and her robe has slipped off her shoulder. An attendant comes hurrying up with a receptacle, but alas! she is just

Fig. 10.—An Unfortunate Incident at a Theban Dinner-Party. (*After Wilkinson.*)

too late. Since such an episode as this is not infrequently found depicted on the walls of a tomb-chapel, it was clearly regarded as a trifling affair, the usual occurrence at a feast. So there was no scandal and no horrified pause in the proceedings. The flautists continued to breathe their soft melodies, the harpers still smote the chords, and the dancers leapt more wantonly than ever, while

TEMPLE OF KHONS, KARNAK.
View looking through the pylon to the avenue of sphinxes.
(See p. 62.)

the musicians sang: *Come, songs and music are before thee; set behind thee all cares; think only upon gladness—until the day cometh that thou shalt go to the land which loveth silence.* " Carpe diem " was certainly the motto of the ancient inhabitants of Luxor. It cannot surely now be said that the Egyptians were a dull and gloomy people and that Egyptology is an inhuman study! Nay, the Egyptians were a most cheerful un-Puritanical people. There was indeed no room for Mrs. Grundy when they made merry! No wonder that the wise Ani thought it necessary to warn his son against the evils of alcoholic excess: *Boast not that thou canst drink a pitcher of beer. Thou speakest, and an unintelligible utterance comes from thy mouth. If thou fallest down and breakest thy limbs, there is no one to offer thee a hand. Thy companions in drink stand up and say, "Away with this sot!" If there cometh one to seek thee in order to question thee, he findeth thee lying on the ground and thou art (as helpless) as a little child.*

But the Theban youths seem to have gone their own way, and paid scant heed to the prating old kill-joy! Accordingly we find a teacher writing reproachfully to a fast young scholar of his as follows: *They tell me that thou dost forsake writing, and dost hanker after pleasures. Thou goest from street to street, where (?) it smells of beer, to destruction (?). Beer, it scares men (from thee), it sends thy soul to perdition. Thou art like a broken steering-oar in a ship, that pays no heed to either side. Thou art like a shrine without its god, a house without bread. . . . Thou sittest with the wench and art besprinkled with scent; thy garland of flowers hangs about thy neck and thou drummest on thy paunch. Thou dost reel and (then) fallest face downwards, and art besmirched with dirt.*

So the heedless youths of ancient Egypt were as unwilling to be studious and take the advice of their moralizing elders as are the youths of to-day —and of all ages and all countries.

CHAPTER II

HOW THEBES BECAME THE CAPITAL OF EGYPT

DURING the Fourth Dynasty, that is to say the earlier part of the period known as the Old Kingdom, a period of about 400 years—2900 B.C. to 2475 B.C., according to the usually accepted dating —the power of the Pharaoh was absolute; the government of the country was entirely vested in him, even the office of vizier being held by his eldest son. Under the kings of the Fifth Dynasty this absolutism of the Pharaoh underwent some modification. A new family, probably assisted by other noble families, attained the kingly power, and one of the resulting changes was that the office of vizier was no longer the perquisite of the crown prince, but was bestowed upon a distinguished subject. Breasted has suggested that some sort of bargain was made between the heads of the two most influential families in Egypt, by which the one received the crown and the other the viziership.

During the Fifth Dynasty also the governors of the different provinces into which Egypt was divided began to assert themselves. By the commencement of the Sixth Dynasty, about 2625 B.C., Egypt had developed into a feudal state, the erstwhile local governors having become great nobles, each firmly entrenched in his own domain and exercising an hereditary claim upon it. Under a strong energetic monarch like Piōpi I. the new system would have seemed harmless enough, for the local barons supplied him with all the troops and artisans he required for his expeditions and for the execution of public works. But the evil side of the system immediately became manifest under a weak sovereign. Piōpi II., the last king of the Sixth Dynasty of whom anything positive is known, ascended the throne at the age of six and reigned for at least ninety years. During the latter part of his reign his grasp on the sceptre doubtless slackened and the power of the feudatories grew apace. Piōpi II.'s immediate successors seem to have been too weak to keep their vassals in order, as were also the shadowy kings of the two next dynasties, the Seventh and the Eighth, who are said to have been descendants of the old royal house, and to have still retained Memphis as their capital.

Here they may have reigned, but certainly did not rule, for Egypt broke up into a collection of small states, governed by petty princes, who, formerly the Pharaoh's obedient vassals, now fought incessantly with one another and with their nominal overlord.

The barons, who were continually engaged in private war, naturally could not keep order in their domains, and crime was everywhere rife. The state of affairs is thus described in a remarkable literary composition of this period, the so-called " Admonitions of an Egyptian Sage":* *Men sit over the bushes until the benighted traveller comes, in order to plunder his load. What is upon him is taken away. He is beiaboured with blows of the stick and slain wrongfully.* Under such conditions arts and crafts were neglected and decayed. *No craftsmen work; the enemies of the land have spoilt its crafts.* Ipuwer, the author of these "Admonitions," describes the prevailing anarchy and consequent topsy-turvydom in picturesque fashion. *The land*, he exclaims, *turns round as does a potter's wheel.* The whole social order had been subverted, and accordingly we are informed that *all female slaves*

* A. H. Gardiner, "The Admonitions of an Egyptian Sage," Leipzig, 1909.

are free with their tongues. When their mistress speaks it is irksome to the servants. Again: *Good things are in the land, yet mistresses of noble houses say, " Would that we had something to eat !"* Yet again we read: *Great ladies, who were mistresses of goodly things, give their children in exchange for beds. The children of princes are dashed against walls. The offspring of desire are laid out on the high ground. . . . The poor man is full of joy. Every town says, " Let us suppress the powerful among us."* This is Bolshevism four thousand years before Lenin and Trotsky !

It was, of course, a great time for the clever and unscrupulous speculator, and this ancient Egyptian revolutionary period produced its crop of *nouveaux riches* as well as its "new poor." *He who once possessed no property is now a man of wealth. The poor of the land have become rich. He who had no dependants is now a lord of serfs. . . . He who never built for himself a boat is now a possessor of ships. He who once possessed them looks at them, but they are not his.*

Taking advantage of the internal disorders prevailing throughout the country, a horde of Asiatics —called 'Aamu (see Fig. 11) by the Egyptians— invaded Egypt and occupied the Delta, a calamitous event that is described by Ipuwer as follows: *The Desert (i.e., the desert-dwellers) is throughout the land. The provinces are laid waste. A foreign tribe from abroad has come to Egypt.* Ipuwer tells us how the Delta is overrun by the Asiatics: *The*

Fig. 11.—A Party of 'Aamu.
(*After* Newberry, "*Beni Hasan.*")

tribes of the desert have replaced the Egyptians everywhere. Nowhere are there Egyptians. . . . Behold the Delta is in the hands of those who know it not as those who once knew it. The Asiatics are now skilled in the arts of the Marshlands.

Trade with abroad was, of course, at a standstill. *No longer*, laments the sage, *do men sail north-*

ward to Byblos.* *What shall we do then for cedars for our mummies, with the produce of which priests are buried, and with the oil of which chieftains are embalmed as far off as Crete ? They come no more. Gold is lacking . . . all handicrafts are at an end.*

Towards the end of the work Ipuwer laments that Rēʻ, the sun-god and creator, the prototype of all earthly kings, had suffered mankind to multiply upon the earth, and had not, when he saw men's evil nature, suppressed them once and for all and prevented the propagation of further trouble and sin : *It is said (of Rēʻ) that he is the herdsman of all men ; there is no evil in his heart. When his herds are few he passes the day to gather them together. . . . But would that he had perceived men's nature in the first generation, then he would have suppressed evil ; he would have stretched forth his hand against it. But men desired to give birth, and so sadness grew up and needy people on every side.* Ipuwer then bewails the fact that there is now no earthly king who, in his capacity of son of Rēʻ, might, a very god incarnate, restore order and bring prosperity again to a distracted nation : *There is no pilot. Where is he to-day ? Doth he sleep perchance ? Behold, his might is not seen.*

* A Syrian port at the foot of Lebanon

SACRED LAKE, KARNAK.
Ceremonial voyages of Amun and co-templar divinities took place on its waters.

Two of these Seventh to Eighth Dynasty kings, Neferkauḥōr and Neferirkerēʿ II., have left records showing that their authority was recognized in Upper Egypt. But this authority was quite transitory. After the lapse of some years, during which time baron waged war on baron, the powerful lords of Herakleopolis, the modern Ehnāsīyeh el-Medīneh, gradually fought their way to a position of authority, and at last one of them was able to assume the Pharaonic titulary, becoming the founder of the line of kings comprising the Ninth and Tenth Dynasties. The Herakleopolitans maintained their supremacy, perhaps, for some hundred years or more, their monuments being found as far south as Coptos, and even at the first cataract. But after that another noble family came to the fore, the barons of the Thebaid, whose original home was Hermonthis, the modern Erment, but who at an early stage in their upward career made their headquarters at Thebes. They were the ancestors of the Eleventh and Twelfth Dynasty kings, and laid the foundations of the Theban hegemony which was to last for more than a thousand years.

When we are once more in possession of a consecutive series of historic documents, we find that the power of the Herakleopolitan Pharaohs is on the decline and that they and their Theban vassals are contending for the supremacy.

During the period of the Herakleopolitan domination, despite the foreign occupation of the Delta and continual warfare with the south, art and especially literature seem to have flourished; indeed, some of the most remarkable Egyptian literary works that we possess appear to date from this age. The art is distinguished by a remarkable naturalism, similar to that which characterizes the reliefs and paintings, of a somewhat later date, which decorate the tomb-chapels of the feudal lords of Cusæ,* a domain that was well within Herakleopolitan territory. Contemporary decorated tomb-chapels of the barons of Asyūṭ also exist, indicative of the prosperity and wealth of this district and period. The reliefs decorating these last-mentioned tomb-chapels, however, are crude as compared with the characteristic work of the Herakleopolitan sculptors, their style for some reason or other being akin to that of the more or less contemporary productions of the Theban *ateliers*.

Certain assertions occurring in the inscriptions

* See A. M. Blackman, "The Rock-Tombs of Meir," vols. i.–iv. (London, 1915–23.)

GROWTH OF THEBAN POWER 43

which are to be found in these Asyūṭ tomb-chapels, indicate, from the fact that they are so very emphatic, that during the decline of the Herakleopolitan ascendancy the state of affairs in many parts of Middle Egypt, outside the Asyūṭ domain, was anything but satisfactory. *Every official was at his post*, we read ; *there was no fighting, nor any shooting an arrow. The child was not smitten beside his mother, nor the citizen beside his wife. There was no evil doer.* Or, again, we are informed that *when night came he who slept on the road gave me* (the feudal lord of Asyūṭ) *praise, for he was like a man in his own house; the fear of my soldier was his protection.*

Some of the inscriptions in these tomb-chapels at Asyūṭ are most important historical documents. One in the tomb-chapel of a certain baron named Tefibi tells us about the campaign which he waged against the Thebans on behalf of his Herakleopolitan overlord King Akhthoi. The baron of the Thebaid was chief of a confederacy of the southern lords, a confederacy which controlled the whole country between Aswān and a city some way north of Abydos, that is between Abydos and Asyūṭ. Tefibi defeated the army of the confederacy and won back to the Pharaoh territory as far south as Abydos. However, this set-back to the rising fortune of the Thebans was not lasting, for they soon regained Abydos and probably a considerable stretch of territory to the north of it as well.

A very interesting literary work of this period, entitled "The Instruction which King Akhthoi made for his son Merikerē'," gives us a lot of valuable information as to contemporary happenings. King Akhthoi speaks of trouble in the Thinite nome or province—the province in which Abydos was situated—and this he ascribes to his own faulty policy. He is here doubtless referring to his final loss of that town; he certainly owns to loss of territory in the southern extremity of his dominions.

Taking advantage of his quarrel with the Thebans, the Asiatics in the Delta appear to have caused Akhthoi considerable trouble. Accordingly, we gather, he made peace with the southern confederacy, acquiesced in his losses, and turned his attention to his northern frontier.

He seems to have inflicted a defeat upon the Asiatics, for in the "Instruction" he mentions that he plundered their cattle and carried off captives. In that same composition his son Merikerē' is advised to strengthen the fortifications of Athribis, the modern Benha, a town not far north of Cairo, a statement showing that during the latter part of the Tenth

Dynasty the Asiatics held practically the whole of the Delta. Merikerēʻ is also advised by his father to build castles along his northern frontier and so protect his territory from further invasion. Akhthoi also recommends his son to be content with what he has got and not attempt reprisals on his southern neighbours. Akhthoi points out that owing to the cessation of hostilities between him and the Thebans, trade between Upper and Middle Egypt has revived, and red granite is being imported from Aswān to the northern capital.

But this advice points only too clearly to the growing weakness of the Herakleopolitan rule, and Merikerēʻ was probably the last of his line to become Pharaoh.

That the Herakleopolitan supremacy was rapidly passing we likewise learn from the inscriptions in the tomb-chapel of Baron Akhthoi of Asyūṭ, who flourished under King Merikerēʻ, the prince to whom King Akhthoi's "Instruction" was addressed. An insurrection broke out and Merikerēʻ had to fly for refuge to his loyal vassal at Asyūṭ, who put down the rebellion and restored the Pharaoh to his throne. After this outburst Baron Akhthoi seems to have passed the rest of his days ruling in peace over his domain.

But this Akhthoï's successors were unable to maintain their resistance against Thebes, and when Asyūṭ finally fell to the forces of the warlike Southerners, the Tenth Dynasty came speedily to an end.

The kings of the Eleventh Dynasty, seven in all, gradually extended their sway, but it was not till Amenemḥēt I., the founder of the Twelfth Dynasty, obtained the throne, that the Asiatics were finally driven out of the Delta. Amenemḥēt, it would seem, was vizier of his immediate predecessor Menthotpe IV., the last king of the Eleventh Dynasty, and he must either have dethroned his royal master or else, what is more likely in view of what we know of his character, contrived, thanks to his high position, to seize the crown at his death.

The accession of Amenemḥēt does not necessarily imply the rise to kingly power of a new family; on the contrary, there is reason to suppose that he belonged to the same royal house, but to a younger branch of it.

The kings of the Eleventh Dynasty, though they had made Thebes their headquarters, were apparently, as already stated, of Hermonthite origin, and they were devoted to Mont, the local divinity of their ancestral home. The family, or branch of

AMENEMḤĒT I. 47

the family, to which Amenemḥēt belonged, had become in a particular sense associated with Thebes, and had a special veneration for Amūn, the god of that city. Since the earthly kingship was vested in a Theban family, the divine kingship naturally was vested in the Theban god, just as it was, as a matter of fact, vested in Khnūm, the god of Herakleopolis, during the rule of the two Herakleopolitan dynasties. Accordingly the Theban Amūn (see Fig. 12), like the Herakleopolitan Khnūm, was identified with the Heliopolitan sun-god, the State-god of Egypt from time immemorial (see below, p. 67), and became Amunrēʻ. Thus under the kings of the Twelfth Dynasty Thebes

Fig. 12. — Amūn of Thebes.

(*After* Erman, "*Handbuch des agyptischen Religion.*")

attained the religious hegemony of Egypt. On the other hand, it was not, as later under the kings of the Eighteenth Dynasty, made the civil capital, though its newly acquired religious importance entitled it to that position. The reason for this was that Amenemḥēt and his successors found that it was politically more suitable to have the centre of administration further north, and accordingly they founded a fortress-city called Ithtōwi, "Seizer of the Two Lands," in the neighbourhood of the modern Lisht and just north of the Fayūm (which became very important during this dynasty), that is to say, halfway between the two previous capitals, Memphis and Herakleopolis.

During the reigns of the first two Amenemhēts and Sesōstrises the feudal system still continued, the barons governing their domains in semi-independence, though rendering dues and service (military and otherwise) to the central government. Under Sesōstris II. the feudal lords reached the height of their wealth, magnificence, and power, and were a serious menace to the reigning house at Ithtōwi. Under such conditions great national undertakings were almost impossible, for the revenues were largely diverted from the central treasury into the pockets of the feudatories.

Sesōstris II.'s successor, Sesōstris III., was a man of immense strength of character, masterful, an able administrator and organizer, and possessed of considerable military ability. He is, in fact, the first Imperialist of whom we have any record. Fully alive to the danger that threatened the

VIII.

COLONNADED COURT, TEMPLE OF LUXOR.
Reliefs on walls largely the work of Tut'cnkhamun. (See p. 64.)

central government at the hands of the overpowerful feudatories, he proceeded to put an end to the existing order of things and replace the local rulers by salaried officials, nominated and paid by the crown. He thus established a centralized bureaucratic system of government, which, surviving the Hyksōs invasion and domination, lasted on throughout the whole succeeding Imperial Epoch.

This administrative change was made possible by

Fig. 13.—Egyptian Soldiers of the Time of Sesōstris III.
(*After* Newberry, " Beni Hasan.")

Sesōstris III.'s wars in the Sudan, which resulted in a real occupation of that country, probably right up to the fourth cataract. There had hitherto been no standing army, the Pharaoh, when he required soldiers (see Fig. 13), calling upon one or more of his barons to supply them, and often to accompany them and command them in the field. But Sesōstris III., however the troops had been raised in the first instance, commanded them in person and himself arranged the plan of campaign. By so doing he gained the confidence and control of the soldiers, who must soon have begun to transfer to him the allegiance they owed to the feudatories. The king thus forged a weapon with which he was not only able to smite and subdue the Sudanese, but put down the semi-regal independence of the nobles. During his reign we see the hereditary territorial ruler becoming, or being replaced by, the town-mayor, while the host of officials that once thronged the local magnate's court and administered his domain became responsible only to the central authority at Ithtōwi.

The feudatories once abolished, the king had the entire resources of the country at his disposal, and he promptly proceeded to utilize them for enterprises of national utility. Forts were erected at strategic points in Nubia, temples were built, or enriched with gold utensils and statuary.

Sesōstris III., however, was largely occupied with wars in the south and in organizing his newly acquired territory and his newly instituted bureaucracy. It was his successor, Amenemḥet III., who carried out those immense engineering and architectural undertakings, which were the glory of the period and marked the apogee of Middle Kingdom magnificence.

THE HYKSŌS INVASION 51

After the death of this last-mentioned Pharaoh the power of the dynasty rapidly declined, and the country was once more plunged into the state of disorder and civil strife that had prevailed when Amenemḥēt I. had seized the reins of government some two hundred years previously.

Professor Eduard Meyer thinks that the feudal barons, who had seemingly been crushed out of existence by the strong Sesōstris III. and Amenemḥēt III., were, owing to the weakness of the latter's successor, Amenemḥēt IV., once again able to raise their heads, engineer a successful rebellion, and avenge themselves on the family of their former subjugators by bringing the dynasty to an end. Thereupon, as after the fall of the Sixth Dynasty, baron waged war on baron, and one usurper fought his way to the throne only to be hurled from it by another. Moreover, now as then, a horde of Asiatics poured into the Delta, where they not only maintained their position for over a hundred years, but at one time extended their sway over the whole or Egypt. These Asiatic conquerors, the Egyptian historian Manetho tells us, were called Hyksōs by his countrymen, a word meaning " shepherd- " or more properly " herdsman-kings." Manetho also relates that the Hyksōs effected the conquest of the country "without a battle," and that they were savage and cruel. The ease with which the Egyptians were overcome and subdued is not only to be explained by the fact that the land was in a state of turmoil due to the breakdown of the central government and the existence of civil strife, but also to the invaders possessing a new, and to the Egyptians terrifying, engine of war—the horse-chariot. Till that time, it must be borne in mind, no wheeled vehicles and no horses had ever been seen in the Nile Valley.

The regular Egyptian troops consisted of infantrymen armed with large heavy shields, battle-axes and spears, and the kind of fighting in which they excelled was the pitched battle in massed formation (Fig. 14). The Asiatic archers could dash hither and thither in their chariots, pour a hail of arrows on the massed Egyptian troops, and at the same time avoid hand-to-hand fighting, in which the Egyptians would doubtless have had the better of them. Such tactics would have inflicted heavy losses on the Egyptians and at the same time have had a most demoralizing effect upon them, for they would have been quite unable to retaliate. Their enemy's losses, on the other hand, would have been comparatively slight. When once panic had

THE HYKSŌS INVASION

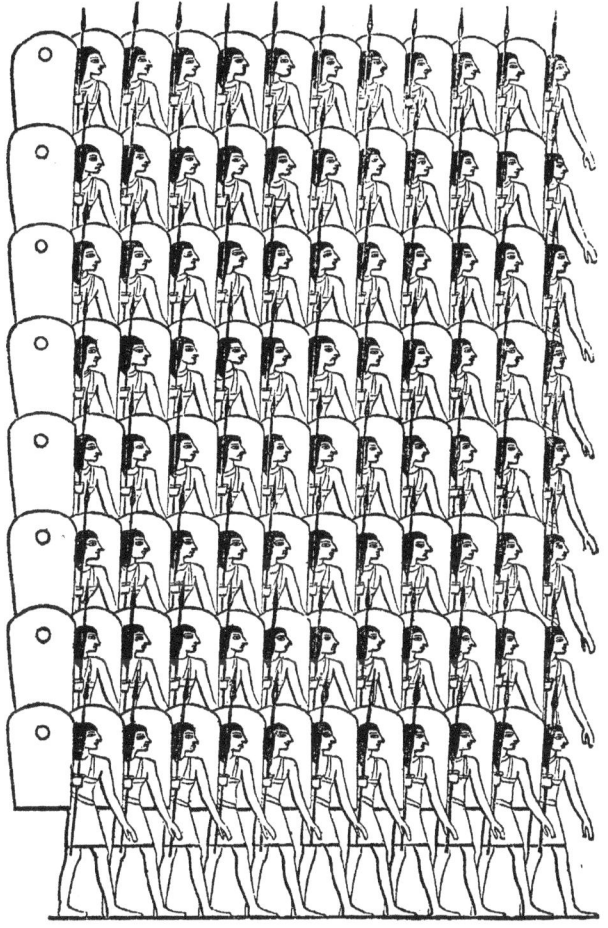

Fig. 14.—Egyptian Heavy-armed Troops.
(*After Wilkinson.*)

seized upon the Egyptians and their serried ranks had been shattered, the enemy archers dashing in and out among them in pursuit would have completed their demoralization. After one or two such engagements the Asiatics would have permanently established their moral superiority, and the Egyptian spirit of resistance would have been utterly broken. Doubtless what Manetho meant by the words " without a battle " was that nothing in the nature of what the Egyptians were accustomed to regard as a battle had been fought, that is a hand-to-hand battle between opposing masses of heavy-armed troops.

The Hyksōs established their headquarters at Avaris, a fortress-city probably built on the same site as that occupied later by the Nineteenth Dynasty city of Pi-Ra'messe, "House of Ramesses," the Pelusium of the Greeks. From here they ruled over the whole of the Delta, and also exercised authority over Upper Egypt, where a native dynasty, with its capital at Thebes, continued to exist in a state of vassalage to the Asiatics.

During the latter half of the Hyksōs domination, which is supposed to have lasted for over a hundred years, the native kings at Thebes were constantly attempting, with varying fluctuations of success and reverse, to assert their independence.

The body of one of these Theban kings, a certain

Seḳenenrē', is preserved in the Cairo Museum. This king was evidently slain in the thick of a fight. A blow from a battle-axe has cleft his left cheek, laying bare the teeth and splitting the jaw-bone. Another blow from the same weapon has penetrated deep into the skull, so that the brain has exuded over the forehead. There is also a wound above the right eye, probably the work of a dagger or spear, and the teeth have bitten through the tongue in the death agony.

Probably this Seḳenenrē' is the native king mentioned in the tantalizingly fragmentary folk-tale, which relates how the Hyksōs suzerain at Avaris sought the occasion of a quarrel with his vassal at Thebes, sending him a messenger to inform him that his overlord's sleep at Avaris was disturbed by the noise of the hippopotami in a pond at Thebes—*they permit me no sleep, day and night the noise of them is in my ears.* Evidently the Hyksōs king was successful in his attempt, and the fighting ended disastrously for the Thebans, for not only was Seḳenenrē' slain in battle, but, at the beginning of his successor Kamōse's reign (see below, pp. 84 foll.), the Hyksōs held the country as far south as Cusæ. There is reason to suppose that previously the Theban dominion had extended as far north as Eshmunēn, so evidently the fighting that cost the Thebans the life of their king also caused them a considerable territorial loss as well.

But, as we shall see in Chapter IV., under Kamōse's leadership the tide turned definitely in favour of the Thebans, and the war of liberation was finally brought to a triumphant conclusion by Aḥmōse I., the founder of the Eighteenth Dynasty.

Under the kings of the Twelfth Dynasty Thebes had become the religious centre of Egypt, its god Amūn being identified with Rēʿ-Atum of Heliopolis, and so attaining the position of state-god. Aḥmōse not only restored to Thebes its religious hegemony, but also made it the capital city of the newly re-founded Empire. Except for the greater part of the reign of Akhenaton, who for religious reasons made his capital at El-Amarna in Middle Egypt, Thebes retained this great position unchallenged till the end of the dynasty—namely, for more than two hundred years. Even during the Nineteenth and Twentieth Dynasties, that is to say during a period of two hundred and fifty years, when for strategical reasons Pi-Raʿmesse became the residential city of the Pharaohs, Thebes still

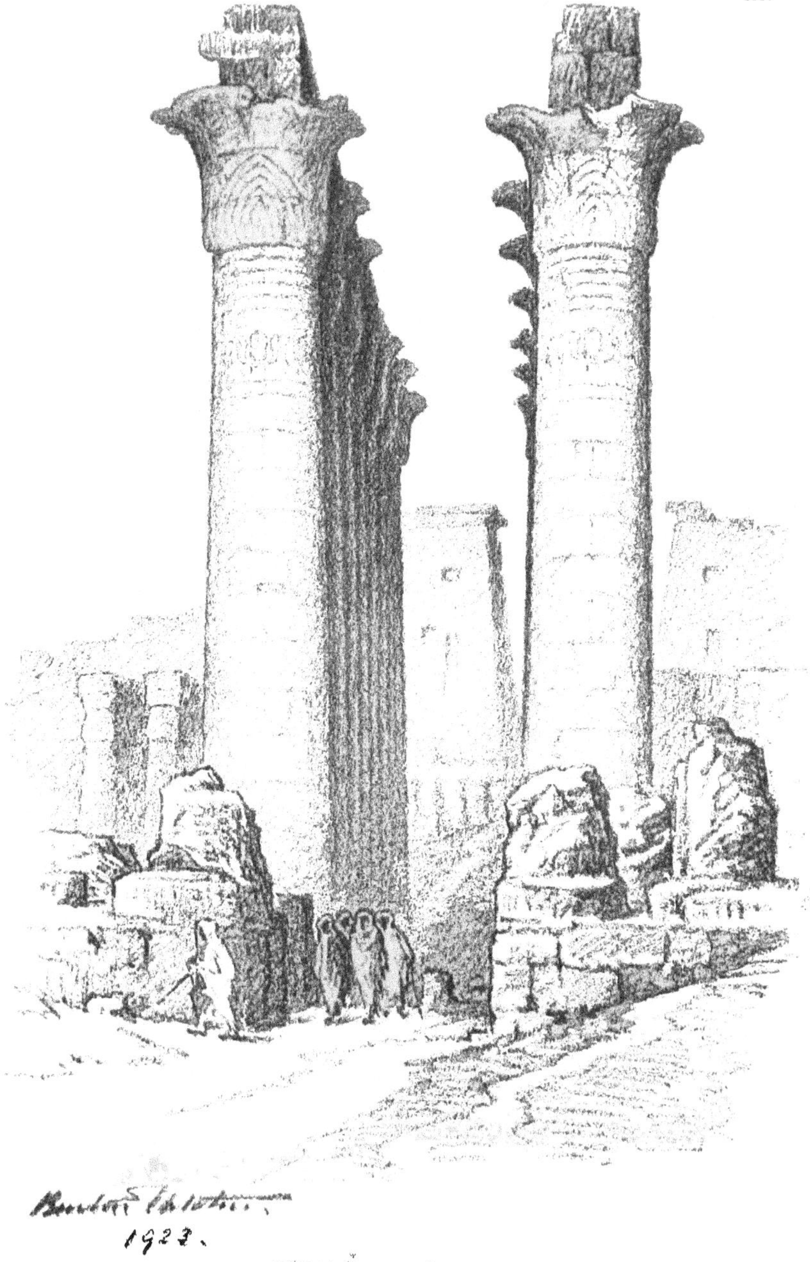

HYPOSTYLE HALL, TEMPLE OF LUXOR.

remained the religious capital of the Empire, and also in many respects the civil capital also. Thus for well over four hundred years Thebes may be said to have been the chief centre of civilization, the world's imperial city.

CHAPTER III

THEBES, THE WORLD'S FIRST MONUMENTAL CITY

As has been pointed out in the foregoing chapter, the real greatness of Thebes—not inaptly called by Professor Breasted the world's first monumental city — only dates from the beginning of the Eighteenth Dynasty, when Aḥmōse, after driving the Hyksōs out of Egypt, made that city the administrative as well as the religious centre of the reconstructed kingdom. But from his time onwards every Pharaoh of the Imperial Age added to its splendours, building a new temple, or adding to or reconstructing one that already existed, setting up a towered gateway here, or splendid statues, or obelisks, there. The great temple of Amūn at Karnak alone has ten such gateways, not including those of the smaller temples grouped around it. Thebes, therefore, well deserved the epithet "hundred-gated" assigned it by the poet Homer.

Part of a building at Karnak erected by the famous Ḏhutmōse III., about whom more will be said in Chapter IV., is shown on Plate III. The

BUILDINGS OF DHUTMŌSE III.   59

two granite pillars which once helped to support the roof are of unusual beauty and design. One displays the lily, the badge of Upper, and the other the papyrus, the badge of Lower Egypt.

Not far off lies the great festival hall of the same king, measuring one hundred and forty-four feet in

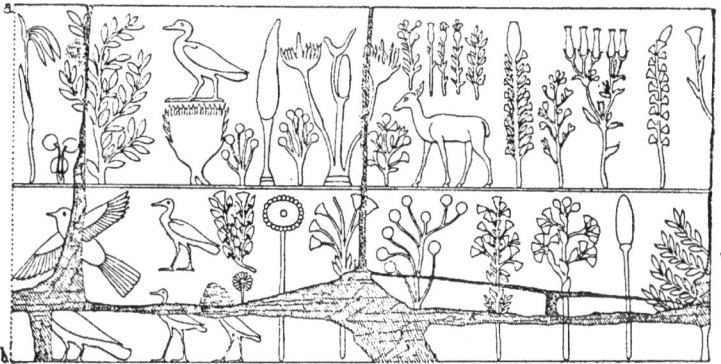

Fig. 15.—Some of the Botanical and Zoological Specimens brought to Egypt by Dhutmōse III.
(*After Mariette,* "*Karnak.*")

width and fifty-two in depth. The roof is supported on twenty columns in two rows and thirty-two square pillars, which divide the building into five aisles. The columns are shaped like tent-poles, and it was evidently the architect's intention to reproduce in stone a huge tent, such as is still erected in modern Egypt on the occasion of festivals for the reception of guests and for the performance of religious ceremonies therein. Attached to this hall are a number of rooms, in one of which are the well-known representations of trees, plants and animals (see Fig. 15) which Ḏhutmōse III. brought back from Palestine after his third campaign, and placed in a combined botanical and zoological garden.

Magnificent as were the architectural achievements of the Eighteenth Dynasty Pharaohs at Karnak, they were completely surpassed by those of Seti I. and Ramesses II. of the succeeding Dynasty, whose gigantic columned hall (see Plates IV. and V.) ranks as one of the wonders of the world. This hall is one hundred and seventy feet long and three hundred and thirty-eight feet wide, and it covers an area of six thousand square yards. The roof was upheld by one hundred and thirty-four columns, arranged in sixteen rows. The columns in the two central rows are higher than the rest, and their capitals represent the fully expanded umbels of the papyrus plant, while those in the other rows have bud-capitals. The two central rows of columns forming the nave are seventy-nine feet high. The roof of the nave is higher than that of the aisles on either side—the columns there being only forty-six feet high—thus enabling the hall to be lit by clerestory windows

GREAT COLUMNED HALL AT KARNAK 61

filled with stone gratings (see Fig. 16). The walls, ceilings, and columns of the hall are decorated with inscriptions and reliefs, all once brilliantly coloured. Even now, though partially ruined and with its colouring vanished or dimmed by age, the building

Fig. 16.—Great Columned Hall at Karnak.
(*After Maspero, "Archéologie égyptienne."*)

is extraordinarily impressive; but in its pristine condition it must have been overwhelmingly magnificent.

Not only the interiors of Egyptian temples were decorated with painted reliefs and inscriptions, but all the outer walls as well, and also the towered gateways. In fact, the public buildings of Thebes, temples and palaces alike, must literally have blazed with colour.

Some idea of the brilliance and magnificence of Imperial Thebes is conveyed to us by certain passages in an inscription of Amenhotpe III., describing a great towered gateway or pylon which he erected, that now known as the third Karnak pylon, and standing behind the great hall of Seti I. and Ramesses II. just described. We are told that two stelæ of lapis-lazuli were set up, one on either side of the entrance, and that the door itself was overlaid with gold and encrusted with lapis-lazuli and precious stones. The floor was overlaid with silver, and the flag-staffs fastened to the face of either tower (see below, p. 66) overlaid with gold, so that they *shone more than the heavens.* In front of the pylon, to which an avenue of sphinxes led up from the river, was erected a colossal statue of Amenhotpe, twenty cubits in height. A similar avenue of sphinxes, be it noted, also the work of Amenhotpe III., connected Karnak and Luxor temples (see Plate VI.) which are about a mile and a half apart, and yet another, the work of Haremheb, led from the temple of Amūn's consort Mut to the tenth pylon of the temple of Amūn himself.

TEMPLE LAKES AND GARDENS

An important and beautiful adjunct of the temple of Karnak, as indeed of every Egyptian temple, was the sacred lake (see Plate VII.), upon which, at certain festivals, boats containing images of the gods were made to go on ceremonial voyages. The banks of such lakes, we are informed, were planted with trees, and in the water grew blue and white lotus flowers. The temple of Mut was half surrounded by its sacred lake, and on the mirror-like surface of the water every feature of the building, its many statues, its walls, its towered gateways, were perfectly reproduced.

The precincts of an Egyptian temple were not only beautified by a tree-encircled pool, but a considerable part was laid out as a garden *planted with all flowers* (see Fig. 45 on p. 177). Such a garden was that made by Dhutmōse III. (see above) when he returned from his third victorious campaign, and the famous *Papyrus Harris*, which enumerates the benefactions of Ramesses III., contains many allusions to the temple gardens which that king either created or restored. Thus we are told that the temple of Amūn at Pi-Ra'messe *was furnished with large gardens and promenades, with all sorts of date-groves bearing their fruits, and a sacred avenue brightened with the flowers of every land.*

After that vast conglomeration of buildings, the temple of Amūn at Karnak, the most magnificent structure in Egypt is surely the temple of Luxor. The name by which it was more usually known to the ancient Thebans was *Ipet-Isut* (Elect of Places), but it also bore the designation of *Southern Ḥarīm of Amun*. This temple, as we now know it, is mostly the work of Amenhotpe III., the Louis XIV. of ancient Egypt. Early in his reign, about 1410 B.C., he pulled down the old temple, which dated from the time of the Twelfth Dynasty, about 2000-1800 B.C., and erected in its place a new sanctuary and the usual surrounding chambers, which latter consist of the sanctuaries of the co-templar divinities and rooms in which special ceremonies were performed, or in which the sacred vessels and vestments were stored. In front of this building he constructed a columned hall, later adding a magnificent colonnaded forecourt—the finest in Egypt. Even in their decay the colonnades (see Plate VIII.) still impress one with their beauty, and they form one of the fairest visions ever conjured up by an architect's imagination, and materialized by him in enduring stone.

Amenhotpe III. also began to build in front of his great forecourt yet another pillared hall, a colossal

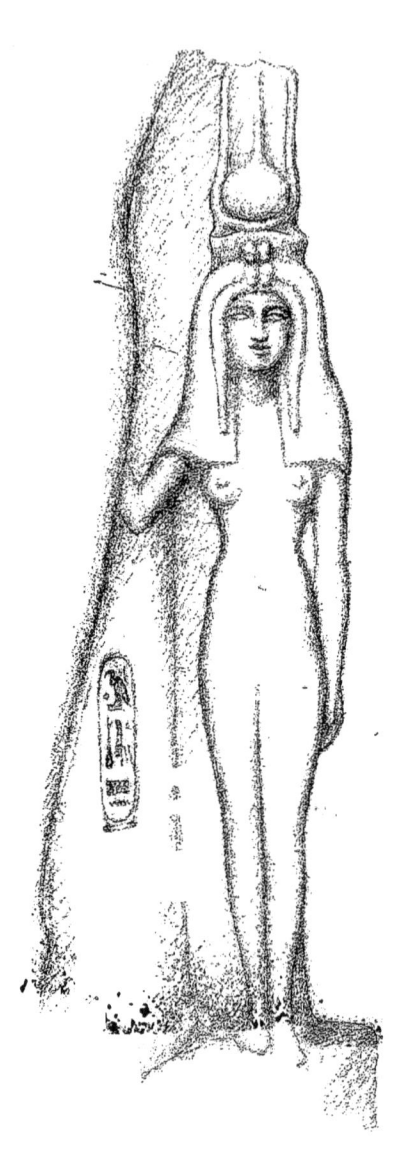

structure. But alas! this great undertaking was never carried out, for the Pharaoh died and none of his successors attempted to complete the work. Only the central aisle was finished, the magnificent sandstone columns of which (see Plate IX.), the tallest hitherto erected in Egypt, tower above the rest of the temple.

These columns of the central aisle, fourteen in number, their capitals representing the outspread flowery umbel of the papyrus plant, are no less beautiful than they are tall, the proportions being perfect. They would have been considerably taller than the columns supporting the roof of either of the side aisles, so that the hall would have been lit by grated clerestory windows, as is the great hypostyle hall of Seti I. and Ramesses II. at Karnak.

In front of the unfinished hall Ramesses II. constructed a very large colonnaded court, to which admittance was gained by a great pylon. Before this pylon, which is decorated with reliefs illustrative of Ramesses' war with the Hittites, were set up six colossal statues of that Pharaoh, two sitting and four standing, and in front of them again two pink granite obelisks, one of which has been removed and re-erected in the Place de la Concorde in Paris.

On the face of each tower of the pylon are to be seen the vertical grooves for the reception of the tall wooden masts, a feature of every Egyptian temple—from the tops of which fluttered blue, green, white, and red flags (see Fig. 17).

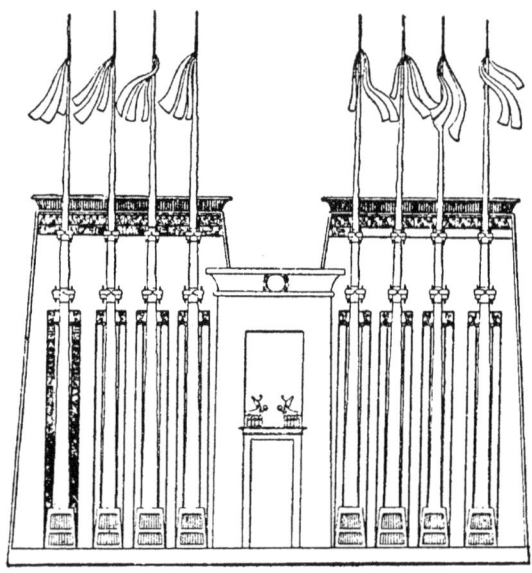

Fig. 17.—A Pylon with its Flag-Staffs.
(*After* Wiedemann, "*Das alte Agypten*".)

The south end of Ramesses II.'s court is decorated with standing colossi of that king, arranged between the columns in the first row. All except one, which is of black granite, are executed in red granite, and they all are about twenty-three feet high. On either side of the doorway leading from

THE PHARAOH'S DIVINE PARENTAGE 67

this court into the unfinished hall of Amenḥotpe III. is erected a seated colossal statue of the king in red granite, with his beautiful queen Nefretiri standing beside him (see Plate XIV.).

It has already been stated that the temple of Luxor bore as an additional name that of *Southern Ḥarīm of Amūn*, a name requiring some explanation, which may well be given at this juncture.

The idea prevailed among the ancient Egyptians that the Pharaoh was the actual physical son of the sun-god Rēʻ-Atum, the god of the city of Heliopolis, the capital of Egypt in pre-dynastic times. Owing to the great influence, religious and political, exercised by Heliopolis on the rest of Egypt, Rēʻ-Atum became for all time the Egyptian State-god, and was regarded both as the first king of Egypt and also as the prototype of all subsequent kings. The Pharaoh was not only considered to be the son of the sun-god, but was also the embodiment of that god on earth. Accordingly when Thebes became the capital of Egypt and the Theban Amūn was identified with Rēʻ-Atum, the Pharaoh was regarded as the son and earthly embodiment of Amūn.

The wife of the ancient king of Heliopolis was high-priestess of Rēʻ-Atum, and in this capacity, and also in that of wife of the sun-god's embodiment, was identified with the goddess Ḥatḥor, the sun-god's wife. She was therefore regarded as earthly consort of that god, and it was through her that he became the physical father of the Pharaoh. Later, when Amūn was identified with the sun-god and consequently attained the position of State-god of Egypt, the Theban Pharaoh's wife became Amūn's earthly wife and was designated *God's Wife of Amūn.*

Incorporating himself in the reigning Pharaoh the sun-god, or the god Amūn identified with him, had intercourse with the queen and so begat the heir to the throne. How this took place is narrated by the priestly scribes of the Imperial Age in the following words: *This august god Amūn, lord of the Thrones of the Two Lands (i.e., Karnak), came, when he had made his mode of being the majesty of this her husband, the king of Upper and Lower Egypt N.* They (*i.e.*, the combination of god and king) *found her as she slept in the beauty of her palace. She awoke because of the savour of the god, and she laughed in the presence of his majesty. He came to her straightway. He was ardent for her. He gave his heart unto her. He let her see him in his form of a god, after he came before her. She rejoiced on beholding his beauty; his love it went*

AMŪN'S HUMAN WIFE AND CONCUBINES 69

through her body. The palace was flooded with the savour of the god, all his odours were as (those of) Punt. Then the majesty of this god did all he desired with her. She let him rejoice over her. She kissed him. . . .*

An important feature in the cult of Amūn of Thebes, in the first instance of the Heliopolitan sun-god, were the performances of musician-priestesses, who danced, sang, beat their single-membrane drums, and shook their sistra or ceremonial rattles in his honour, both in processions and during the celebration of the temple liturgy. When thus engaged, they consciously impersonated Ḥathor, the wife of Rēʿ-Atum, and in certain temples, that of Atum at Heliopolis, and Ḥathor at Denderah, they were actually designated *Ḥathors* (see Fig. 18). The queen, as already stated, was the *God's Wife*, and in this capacity was the earthly embodiment of Ḥathor *par excellence.* Naturally enough the musician-priestesses who were sub-

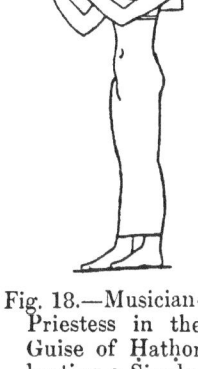

Fig. 18.—Musician-Priestess in the Guise of Ḥathor beating a Single-Membrane Drum. (*After Mariette, "Denderah".*)

---

* See Blackman, " Journal of Egyptian Archæology," vii., p. 17.

ordinate to her, and whom we know to have been attached to the house of the *God's Wife* at Thebes, were, in view of their close association with Ḥathor, regarded as Amūn's (originally the Heliopolitan sun-god's) secondary wives or concubines, the wife of the high-priest of Amūn bearing the title of *Chief of the Concubines.* Luxor Temple, the *Southern Ḥarīm of Amūn*, was probably the headquarters of these concubines, and it was here also possibly that the union of the god and queen was supposed to take place, perhaps on the occasion of the annual New Year's procession (see just below and pp. foll.) to that temple from Karnak. This, if the suggestion is correct, would account for the occurrence in one of the several rooms grouped around the sanctuary of Luxor temple, of a series of reliefs illustrative of the divine conception and birth of the Pharaoh. A similar series, decorating a wall in the temple of Ḥatshepsut at Deir el-Baḥri, will be discussed in Chapter VII.

In a chapter professing to describe some of the glories of ancient Thebes, an account must be given of the great festival of Öpet in honour of Amūn, celebrated annually on New Year's Day, when the god went in solemn procession from his temple at Karnak to his *Southern Ḥarīm* at Luxor.

THE FESTIVAL OF ŌPET

A series of reliefs, occupying the walls on either side of Amenḥotpe III.'s court at Luxor, vividly depicts what took place at this festival. The reliefs were executed during the reign of Tutʿenkhamūn, but were usurped by his next successor but one, Ḥaremḥeb, who everywhere replaced his predecessor's name with his own.

Proceedings began with the presentation of food-and-drink offerings to Amūn, his consort Mut, and their son Khons, in their respective sanctuaries in the great temple of Karnak. The first of the series of the reliefs in question shows us the heaped-up offering tables standing before the shrines containing the images of these three divinities, and Tutʿenkhamūn burning incense in front of one of them, namely that containing the image of Amūn.

The ordinary Egyptian shrine, like those here depicted, was in the form of a boat, which was set on an altar-like stone pedestal, the place in the sanctuary where the pedestal stood being designated *the great place*. In the centre of the boat-shrine, covered with a veil, was the cabin containing the image; such an image was as a rule quite small—sixteen inches to four feet in height—and made of wood. Poles were attached to the boat so that it might be carried in procession, the number of priests who supported it varying from eight to twenty-four, or even twenty-six (see Fig. 19). The boat-shrine was undoubtedly in the first instance an accessory of the Heliopolitan sun-cult, for the sun-god was conceived of as voyaging in a ship across the sky by day and through the underworld by night.

Fig. 19.—Boat-Shrine carried by Priests.

(*After Lepsius,* "*Denkmäler aus Aegypten und Aethiopien*".)

It might here be pointed out that the priesthood at every Egyptian temple was divided into four *watches*, or, as the classical writers designated them, *phylæ*. These *watches* are named after the four quarters of a ship, the bow, stern, starboard, and larboard watch, names assigned in mythological

THE FESTIVAL OF ŌPET 73

texts to the four watches into which the crew of the sun-god's celestial ship was divided. It was evidently the priests of the Heliopolitan sun-god who were first divided into four watches bearing these names, for, as already pointed out, the sun-god in particular was associated with a ship or boat, and his priests may well have been regarded as his crew.

Offering having thus been made to the Theban triad, the priests took the sacred boats out of the sanctuaries where they stood, and, raising them up so that the poles rested on their shoulders, carried them out of the temple and down to the river in solemn procession, twenty-four priests supporting each boat. In front of and behind each boat walked a flabellifer (his flabella or ceremonial fan being exactly like those carried beside the Pope on great occasions), and on either side, in addition to the twenty-four priests, walked a pair of officiants clad in panther-skin vestments. At the head of each of the three groups of attendant- and bearer-priests walked a thurifer with a thurible of burning incense. The king himself followed the principal boat-shrine, that of Amūn, on foot. At the head of the whole *cortège* marched a trumpeter and a drummer (Fig. 20).

On reaching the water's edge, the boat-shrines were placed on board large vessels, which were towed by rowing-boats, and also by companies of men on the river bank, until they arrived opposite the temple of Luxor.

The ships on which the shrines were placed were often magnificent in design and decoration. Amenhotpe III. has left us a description of a ship which he caused to be constructed for the conveyance of Amūn on the occasion of ceremonial voyages such as that under discussion. It was fashioned of *new cedar-wood, which his majesty cut upon the hill country of To-Nūter* (Lebanon), *and which was dragged over the mountains of Retenu by the princes of all foreign countries. It is made very wide and long; never was made the like thereof (aforetime). It is overlaid with silver and inwrought with gold throughout. The great shrine* (i.e., the baldachin amidships under

Fig. 20.—Trumpeter and Drummer heading a Religious Procession.

(*After Wilkinson.*)

THE FESTIVAL OF ŌPET

which the smaller boat-shrine was placed) *is of gold, and it fills the land with its brightness.* The bows of the vessel were adorned with *great crowns, their serpents coiling on either side thereof.* The shrine had in front of it flag-staffs overlaid with gold and a pair of obelisks. Round about the shrine were set up small figures of the "souls" of Buto and Nekhen* and also of two musician-priestesses, the so-called *mert*-priestesses of Upper and Lower Egypt, all making jubilation in honour of the divinity within.

As the flotilla of boats made its way up the river, a great accompanying procession of people, in addition to those who held the tow-ropes, marched simultaneously along the east bank, a priest at the head of them chanting a hymn in honour of Amūn. This procession consisted of soldiers armed with spears and shields, a negro drummer and negro dancers who performed all kinds of antics (see Fig. 21), musician-priests and musician-priestesses rattling respectively their castanets and sistra, soldiers carrying standards, two royal horse-chariots, a lute-player, a number of priests belonging to the higher grades of the hierarchy, and a crowd of Theban citizens who sang and clapped their

* See below, p. 117.

hands in time to the music. On arriving opposite Luxor the boat-shrines were taken out of the ships, hoisted on to the shoulders of the priests, and, with the trumpeter and drummer leading the way, were borne in procession into Luxor temple, the musician-priestesses, Amūn's earthly concubines, dancing and rattling their sistra in his honour.

Fig. 21.—Negro Drummer and Dancers.
(*After Wilkinson*.)

Having entered the temple, the divine visitors were presented with a plentiful supply of food-and-drink offerings, which were consecrated and solemnly made over to them by the king himself. Then, in the evening, they and the accompanying *cortège* returned to Karnak by water and river bank in much the same order, and amid the same display of rejoicing, as when they had set out for Luxor in the morning.

Festivals like these were celebrated with a great

deal of eating and drinking and general jollification, and the temples were specially endowed in order to supply the hosts of visitors and worshippers, who flocked thither on such occasions, with the food and liquor wherewith to make merry and be glad in the god's honour.

An ancient inscription describes such a festival in the following terms: *The gods of heaven shout for joy, shout for joy. . . . The Ḥathors*—(*i.e.*, the musician-priestesses impersonating that goddess) *beat their single-membrane drums. . . . The inhabitants are drunk with wine, chaplets of flowers are on their heads. The sailor-folk* (*i.e.*, the crews of the ships that have conveyed the god and his attendant divinities) *walk joyously about, anointed with the finest unguent. All the children rejoice . . . from the rising to the setting of the sun.*

Drunkenness was, it must regretfully be confessed, a characteristically Egyptian conception of happiness and an almost essential part of the rejoicings at a religious festival. This is well borne out in part of a popular Theban song still preserved to us, which runs as follows: *How happy is the temple of Amunrē‘, even she* (*i.e.*, the temple personified as a woman) *that spendeth her days in festivity with the king of gods within her. . . . She is like to a woman drunken, who sitteth outside the chamber, with loosened hair. . . .*

The Egyptians are, and they ever have been, an intensely conservative people, and it is not at all surprising that this festival of Ōpet, despite religious and other changes and the passage of hundreds of years, still survives in Luxor. The western side of the first colonnaded court of Luxor temple, that erected by Ramesses II., is occupied by a mosque to which a school is attached (see Plate XII.), the mosque containing the tomb of the Sheykh Yūsef Abu'l-Ḥaggāg, the local patron saint. Once a year, the fourteenth day of the Muhammadan month of Sha'bān, the festival in honour of this saint is celebrated. A great procession passes through the principal streets of Luxor, stations being made and prayers recited at the domed tombs of various other local saints. The chief feature of this procession is the brightly painted and beflagged boat of Abu'l-Ḥaggāg, placed in a cart to which ropes are attached, and thus dragged by the faithful through the streets. The accompanying procession consists of gaily caparisoned camels, soldiers, members of various religious confraternities, musicians, dancers, *fiḳīhs* reciting the Kurān, and troops of citizens—men, women, and children—all singing a hymn in honour of the saint.*

The close resemblance of the ancient and the modern festivals to one another is most remarkable, and must be something more than a mere coincidence; in either case, it will have been noticed, the composition of the procession is almost identical.

There are, however, two noticeable differences between the ancient and modern methods of celebrating the festival. Firstly, the sacred boat is dragged along on a wheeled cart, not carried high on the shoulders of priestly bearers or towed up and down the river; and secondly, in which respect they show themselves superior to their pagan ancestors, the masses of the people nowadays do not drink to drunkenness.

In the days of the great emperors the wealth of the known world flowed into Egypt. The harbours of the Delta were crowded with ships of every nationality, loaded with merchandise and with the tribute and presents of subject and friendly states. These ships often, too, it appears, sailed right up the Nile to the Theban docks and

* See G. Legrain, "Louqsor sans les Pharaons," Paris, 1914, pp. 81-91.

80 LUXOR AND ITS TEMPLES

there disgorged their cargoes. Furniture overlaid with gold or fashioned of precious woods inlaid with ivory, chariots encrusted with gold and silver, horses of the purest breeds, bronze weapons and

Fig. 22.—Fragment of a Painted Ceiling.
(*After a drawing by the Author from a photograph.*)

armour inlaid with gold, gold and silver vessels of rare design, multicoloured and elaborately patterned fabrics, the choicest produce of the fields, gardens, vineyards, orchards, and pastures of Palestine and Syria, incense, sweet-smelling woods, perfumes, silver and gold from Asia and the Sudan—all these

XII.

NATIVE SCHOOL.
Constructed among the half-buried columns of the great forecourt, Temple of Luxor.

THEBAN PALACES 81

were brought in seafaring ships or by overland caravans to Egypt and the Egyptian capital. We are informed that the solid rings and ingots, into which the precious metals were cast, lay piled up in heaps in the treasuries and were measured out by the bushel.

Such wealth, as was to be expected, considerably affected the lives, tastes, and habits of Pharaoh and subjects alike. The houses of the wealthy, as we saw in Chapter I., were often finely decorated and furnished, but the royal palaces were beautiful in the extreme. A ceiling in a palace of Amenhotpe III. at Thebes displays a flock of pigeons and many large red butterflies winging their way across an azure sky (see Fig. 22). On the floor beneath the artist depicted a pool of water full of lotus flowers, fish, and swimming duck, the action of the birds being splendidly portrayed. Only a fragment of this pavement is preserved, but no doubt, as in the palace of Akhenaton at El-Amarna, the pool was surrounded with reeds, bushes, and flowering plants, amid which cattle gambolled, while above the flowers and bushes flew butterflies, dragon-flies, and gaily plumaged birds (see Fig. 23) Fragments of a wall-painting surviving from the above-mentioned palace of Akhenaton show us a scene of family life, the king and queen seated on chairs, and their children standing at their parents' knees or squatting on brocaded cushions placed on the carpeted floor.

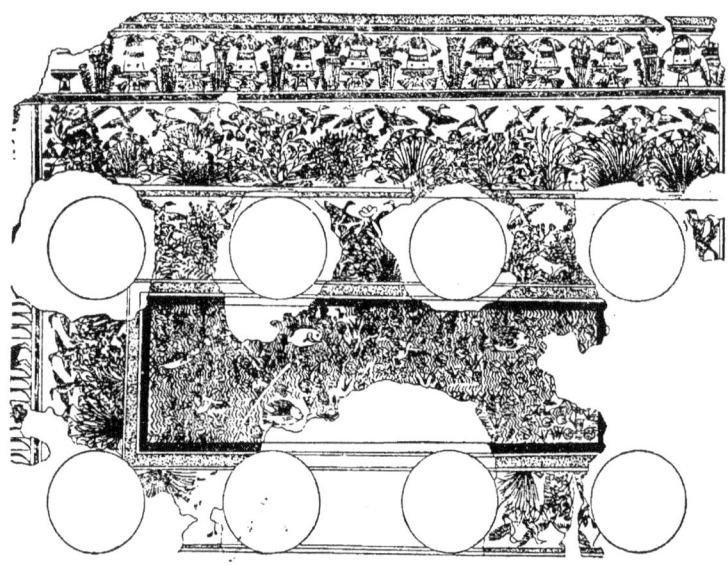

Fig. 23.—Painted Pavement from the Palace of Akhenaton.
(*After* Petrie, "*El-Amarna.*" *By the courtesy of the autho*r.)

The decoration of the columns in many a royal saloon was executed in brilliant glazed inlay as well as in paint, and a great deal of goldfoil was also employed. At El-Amarna this inlay-work took the form of convolvulus plants, or gadding vines, which trail over the shafts of the columns in

THEBES THE MAGNIFICENT 83

riotous profusion, a wonderful adaptation of the realities of nature to the exigencies of design.

In Ramesses III.'s palace at Tell el-Yahūdīyeh in the Delta, now alas! completely destroyed, the walls of some of the apartments, instead of being frescoed, were decorated with glazed plaques. Thousands of rosettes for inlaying, and a number of wonderfully coloured tiles, representing captives of many nations,* are all that survive of a once most beautiful building.

To one passing Thebes on his way up or down the Nile a wonderful panorama must have unfolded itself. For a considerable distance on either bank of the river one temple or palace after another lifted itself up above the trees of the surrounding gardens, the brilliance of the buildings being only enhanced by their green setting. Rising high as the towered gateways, the tapering gold-capped obelisks pointed finger-like at the cloudless sky, and in the blazing sunlight of the orient they shone, as the Egyptians themselves said, *like the sun in the horizon of heaven, so that the two lands are flooded with their rays.*

* See Maspero, "Art in Egypt," London, 1912, plate facing p. 184; also Petrie, "A History of Egypt," iii. (second edition), London, 1918, p. 160.

CHAPTER IV

SOME GREAT KINGS IN TIME OF WAR

ONE of the most interesting documents discovered in recent years is the so-called Carnarvon Tablet No. 1, found by Lord Carnarvon in a plundered tomb at Thebes in the year 1908.* It consists of a wooden board covered on both sides with stucco, and bearing on the obverse face a remarkable historical text, which deals with an episode in the expulsion of the Hyksōs or Shepherd-Kings. The episode in question occurred in the reign of Kamōse, the immediate predecessor of the great Aḥmōse I., the founder of the Eighteenth Dynasty.

The opening passages depict Kamōse sitting in his palace at Thebes and taking counsel with his courtiers and officers. He is described as waxing indignant at the thought that the Asiatics not only occupy the whole Delta, but Upper Egypt as far south as Eshmunēn, while Nubia, which the Theban

* See Alan H. Gardiner in *Journal of Egyptian Archæology*, iii., pp. 95-110; Battiscombe Gunn and Alan H. Gardiner, *op. cit.*, v., pp. 45-48.

kings of the Twelfth Dynasty had conquered and held up to the fourth cataract, is now ruled over by a local chieftain! *To what end am I cognizant of it, this power of mine,* Kamōse bitterly exclaims, *when one prince is in Avaris* (the Lower Egyptian capital of the Hyksōs) *and another in Nubia, while I sit in league with an Asiatic and a negro —each man with his slice of this Egypt? . . . Behold, he* (the Asiatic foe) *holds Eshmunēn, and no man is at ease, wasted through servitude to the Syrians.*

Such a situation was unendurable to Kamōse. *I will grapple with him,* he cries, *and rip open his belly ; my desire is to deliver Egypt and to smite the Asiatics.* But *the great men of his council* urge caution. They are all for safety, and they point out on the one hand how strong the enemy is, and on the other hand that, after all, their position is not as intolerable as the Pharaoh has represented, for *Elephantine* (the modern Aswān) *is strong, and the middle part* (*of Egypt*) *is with us as far* (*north*) *as Cusæ;** also they are permitted to cultivate lands outside their own domain, and they can send their cattle to pasture in the Delta. No, they maintain, let things be, and only fight if attacked.

* The modern El-Ḳuṣīyeh in Asyūṭ province.

This counsel of " safety first " found no favour with the patriotic Pharaoh. We are told that these advisers *were displeasing in the heart of his majesty. . . .* [*Behold, I will fight*] *with the Asiatics. Success will come. . . . The entire land* [*shall acclaim me the powerful ruler*] *within Thebes, Kamōse, the protector of Egypt.*

The king accordingly decided on a forward policy, and, says he, *I sailed down stream as a champion to overthrow the Asiatics by the command of Amūn . . . my army being valorous in front of me like a blast of fire.*

Kamōse evidently took the enemy by surprise, for he succeeded in shutting up the Hyksōs army under the command of a certain Teti, probably the son of the Hyksōs king, in the town of Nefrusi, just north of Eshmunēn, and cutting off their retreat. Having accomplished this, *I spent,* he says, *the night in my ship, my heart being glad.*

The attack delivered next day was completely successful. *When day dawned I was on him as it were a hawk. . . . I overthrew him, I destroyed his wall, I slew his folk, I caused his wife to go down to the river bank* (so as to take her back in triumph to Thebes in one of his galleys). *My troops were like lions with their spoil, with slaves, herds, fat, and* honey, dividing up their possessions, their hearts being glad.

By such vigorous action as this Kamōse played his part in the great and protracted struggle for the liberation of Egypt.

Kamōse's successor Aḥmōse carried on and brought to a successful conclusion the work of clearing the Hyksōs out of Egypt. This accomplished, he invested Sharuhen in Judah, where the Asiatics had entrenched themselves, and, having taken the city after a six-years' siege, finally destroyed any hopes they may have entertained of reconquering the country they had been so ignominiously compelled to evacuate.

Ḏhutmōse I., the third king of the Eighteenth Dynasty, was a hard-bitten campaigner like Aḥmōse, the founder of that line. In the second year of his reign he led his army into Nubia to punish the turbulent desert tribesmen in the southern half of the province, who had started to attack and plunder the Egyptian fortresses and trading settlements which had been established on either bank of the Nile from Aswān to some distance south of the second cataract.

The expedition set out from Thebes in ships, and arrived at the first cataract some time in February, or early in March, only to find that the canal through the cataract had become blocked with stones. As immediate action was urgent, Dhutmōse was not willing to wait while the canal was being reopened. Accordingly his admiral, Aḥmōse by name, forced a passage through the rapids. Later on in the voyage, as we learn from his biography, inscribed on the walls of his tomb-chapel at El-Kāb, Aḥmōse again distinguished himself. *I showed bravery in his* (the king's) *presence in the bad water, in the passage of the ship through the cataract*—(*i.e.*, the second cataract).

In early April somewhere between the second cataract and Tangur—Tangur lies about seventy-five miles south of the cataract—a battle took place, in which, Admiral Aḥmōse tells us, the king engaged a rebel Nubian chieftain in hand-to-hand combat. *His Majesty was enraged thereat like a panther. His Majesty shot, and his first arrow stuck in the neck of that fallen one.* The official account, engraved upon a rock on the island of Tombos, which lies just above the third cataract, describes the result of this expedition in the following terms: *He hath overthrown the chief of the Nubians; the negro is limp and weak by reason of his grip. . . . The Nubian nomads have fallen for*

THE NILE AT LUXOR.

SOME GREAT KINGS IN TIME OF WAR 89

fear, thrown down throughout their lands; their stench, it fills their valleys. Their mouths are (dis) coloured (with blood) like (the spouts of) rain-gutters.

On Tombos Dhutmōse built a fort and furnished it with a garrison. Thence he returned slowly northward, reorganizing and inspecting the country, the Nubian chief, whom he had slain, hanging head downwards at the prow of his ship. When he reached the first cataract he ordered the old canal to be cleared, and sailing through it in triumph—the corpse of the Nubian chief still decorating his galley—proceeded on his way back to Thebes.

The most remarkable account we possess of an Egyptian Pharaoh in time of war is to be found in the so-called Annals of the great Dhutmōse III., who has not inappropriately been designated the Napoleon of the Ancient Orient. These annals, which are engraved on a wall in the temple of Karnak, hard by the beautiful floral columns shown on Plate III., are mere extracts from elaborate records kept by a certain Thanēni and entered by him upon leather rolls. *I followed the king of Upper and Lower Egypt, Menkheperrē̔* (Dhutmōse III.), Thanēni tells us. *I beheld the victories of the king which he won in every foreign land. . . . I recorded the victories which he won in every foreign land, putting them in writing according to the facts.*

During Dhutmōse's joint reign with that remarkable woman Hatshepsut, about whom more will be said in Chapter V., Egypt seems to have lost her hold on her dominions in northern Palestine and Syria. The local dynasts of these regions, whose subjection had been begun by Aḥmōse, and completed by Amenhotpe I. and Dhutmōse I., became restive under petticoat government, and, forming a coalition under the powerful ruler of Kadesh, they broke into open rebellion. As soon as the queen was dead, Dhutmōse began to prepare for the reconquest of northern Palestine and Syria, and, late in the second year of his sole reign, April 19, 1479 B.C., we find him marching with his army from Tharu, the last Egyptian town on the north-east frontier. Nine days later, April 28, he reached Gaza, a city one hundred and sixty miles distant from Tharu, and proceeding from thence along the Palestinian seaboard, arrived, possibly on May 10, at Yehem, a town some ninety miles distant from Gaza and situated on the southwestern slope of that range of mountains at the northern end of which rises Carmel.

Meanwhile the king of Kadesh, having marshalled

his forces, advanced south to oppose the Pharaoh, and took up his position at Megiddo, a fortress-town in the plain of Esdraelon, on the north-east side of the Carmel ridge.

A day or two after reaching Yehem Dhutmōse heard from his spies that the enemy were at Megiddo in force and intending to make their stand there. Accordingly on May 13, probably early in the morning, he called a council of war. The annals profess to give us some of the actual words which the great king addressed to his officers on this occasion. *Now that wretched enemy of Kadesh, having come and having entered into Megiddo, is there at this moment. He has gathered to himself the chiefs of all the countries that were subject to Egypt as far as Naharin. . . . He has said, so one relates, " I am ready to fight against his majesty* (the king of Egypt) *here in Megiddo." Tell ye me that which is in your hearts.*

Now there were three roads to Megiddo from the place where Dhutmōse held his council of war, one, a dangerous route, which made a straight line for that city by way of 'Arūna, and two other easier, but more roundabout, roads, leading respectively to the north and south of it. Evidently in the course of his speech Dhutmōse had expressed his intention of going by the middle road, for the officers are represented as replying: *How is it possible to go upon this road, which gets narrower? It is reported that the enemy is there, standing upon the outside (of the pass), and they are numerous. Will not horse go behind horse, and the troops of the people* (the infantry) *likewise? Will our vanguard be fighting, while our rearguard waits here in 'Arūna without fighting?* They argue that the Pharaoh should go by one of the two easier roads, and not cause them *to march upon this difficult road.*

This plea for caution appeared to be little short of rank cowardice to Dhutmōse, who blazed forth in indignation: *I swear as Rē' loves me, as my father Amūn praises me, as my nostrils are furnished with life and good fortune, my majesty will proceed upon this 'Arūna road. Let him who will among you go upon these roads whereof ye speak. Let him who will among you go in the following of my majesty. Let them not say among the fallen foe, whom Rē' abhors, " Does his majesty proceed upon another road because he fears us?" That is what they will say.*

Dhutmōse's officers, stung by this rebuke, promptly replied: *May thy father Amūn, lord of*

Karnak, within Luxor, do according to thy desire! Behold, we will follow thy majesty whithersoever thy majesty goeth! The servant is behind his lord.

The council broke up and the king gave the order to advance, and the army reached 'Arūna on the evening of May 13. We are informed that during this march Dhutmōse put himself at the head of his troops, for *his majesty swore an oath, saying:* "*I will not suffer my victorious troops to go forth in front of me in this place.*" Accordingly, *his majesty determined to go forth in front of his troops himself. Every man was made to know where he was to march, horse being behind horse, while his majesty was at the head of his troops.*

During the night of the 13th the Egyptian army encamped at the town of 'Arūna, which lay half-way along the 'Arūna road, but was on the move again early the next day, the king, with a statue of the god Amūn carried beside him, again leading the host. The Egyptians had to proceed in single file along the narrow road, and when the king and the vanguard reached the mouth of the pass, where it opened out into the plain opposite Megiddo, the rearguard was still at 'Arūna. His officers besought Dhutmōse to check his advance till the whole host was clear of the defile. *They said unto his majesty, "Behold his majesty goes forth with his victorious troops, they have filled the valley. Let our victorious lord hearken unto us this once. Let our lord guard for us the rear of his troops and his people. When the rear of the host comes forth for us, then we will fight these Asiatics, then we shall not be careful for the rear of our host."* Dhutmōse wisely acceded to this request and guarded the approach to the pass, while the main body of the troops filed through the gorge along the narrow mountain road. Just at noon the last of the host had emerged from the pass and the whole body of troops moved forward together, reaching the bank of the river Kina at 7 o'clock. At that season of the year it is still daylight in Palestine, and so there was time for the troops to encamp before darkness fell. The Pharaoh's tent was pitched, and the command was issued to the army: *Prepare yourselves, make ready your weapons, for one is to advance to fight with this wretched foe at daybreak.* Dhutmōse then went to seek repose in his tent, the staff officers and other members of the royal *entourage* were supplied with provisions, while to the sentries on their rounds was addressed the exhortation—*Steady, steady! Watchful, watchful!* A special guard was set about the royal headquarters, and, before the Pharaoh finally lay down to sleep, he was informed that all was quiet in the neighbourhood and all well with the host.

The next day, May 15, the king appeared at dawn, and the army was ordered to cross the valley of the Kina. *His majesty, we are told, proceeded in a chariot of gold, clad in his accoutrements of war, like Horus the valiant, lord of achievement, like Mont of Thebes, his father Amūn strengthening his hands.* After certain manœuvres, by which the Egyptians secured a position which precluded any possibility of the enemy turning their right flank, the armies met in the clash of battle. Ḏhutmōse, we are told, was in the centre, and *he prevailed against them* (the enemy) *at the head of his troops* (see Fig. 24). *When they saw that his majesty was prevailing against them, then they fled in headlong rout to Megiddo with terror-stricken faces. They left their horses and their chariots of gold and silver, and the people drew them up by hoisting* (them) *with their clothes into this city, for the people of this city had shut them out, wherefore they let down clothes to hoist them up into this city.*

Evidently the enemy had encamped between the city and the Egyptian army, having no inten-

96 LUXOR AND ITS TEMPLES

tion of submitting to a siege, for the victorious troops immediately gave themselves up to looting, and so lost the opportunity of taking Megiddo there and then, as the annalist bitterly complains. However, a goodly spoil was obtained; horses,

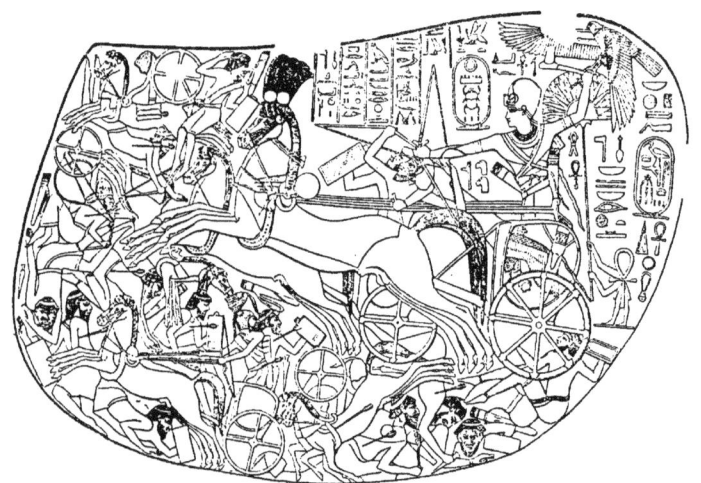

Fig. 24.—An Egyptian King fighting in his Chariot.
(*After Carter-Newberry, " Tomb of Thutmosis IV."*)

chariots of gold and silver, together with the silver-wrought tent of the king of Kadesh, and as for the enemy warriors, we are told that they *lay stretched out like fishes in the corner of a net.*

Having made an inventory of the spoil, the army gave itself up to jubilation and *gave praise to Amūn for the victory which he had given to his*

XIV.

WIFE OF RAMESSES II.
Figure standing beside the colossal statue of the king. (See p. 67.)

SOME GREAT KINGS IN TIME OF WAR 97

son this day, and they cheered the king, extolling his victory.

But what Dhutmōse wanted was neither booty nor cheers, but the capture of Megiddo, and he urged on his army to the assault. He pointed out that all the revolted dynasts were within those walls that confronted them, and of course their capture would mean the smashing of the confederacy once and for all. *It is the capture of a thousand cities, the capture of Megiddo,* he ejaculated. *Capture ye thoroughly, thoroughly!*

However, for some reason or other, no direct assault seems to have been made on the fortress. The Egyptian army beleaguered it instead, surrounding it with earthworks and cutting down all the *pleasant trees* growing in the neighbourhood, either to form a sort of palisade or else to support the heaped-up soil and stones. In course of time, probably after the lapse of a month or so, Megiddo was starved out and surrendered. Also many of the dynasts who had not been shut up within the city walls came and made submission to the Pharaoh. But the king of Kadesh had escaped before Megiddo had been completely invested, and it was not till after four more years of preparatory campaigns that Dhutmōse was able to attain his main objective, the capture of Kadesh, which he accomplished in his sixth campaign, taking it not by siege but by assault.

Amenhotpe II. seems to have been as famous a fighting man as his predecessor, Dhutmōse III., on the receipt of the news of whose death Syria promptly revolted. The energetic Amenhotpe immediately marched against the rebellious dynasts, and, meeting them in battle early in May, 1447 B.C., at Shemesh-Edom, in northern Palestine, gained a great victory. *His majesty*, so the official account of the battle informs us, *furnished an example of bravery there; his majesty himself fought hand to hand. Behold he was like a fierce-eyed lion, smiting the countries of Lebanon.* We learn also, on the same authority, that in this engagement Amenhotpe took with his own hand eighteen prisoners and sixteen horses.

On May 12 he crossed the Orontes, probably at Senzar, and then made for the Euphrates. After making this crossing, Amenhotpe engaged in a hand-to-hand conflict with some enemy chariotry. The already-quoted inscription tells us that *his majesty raised his arm in order to scan the horizon. Then his majesty descried some Asiatics coming on horses (i.e.,* in chariots drawn by horses), *advancing*

SOME GREAT KINGS IN TIME OF WAR 99

at a gallop. Lo, his majesty was decked with his accoutrements of war. . . . They (the Asiatics) *retreated when his majesty looked at one of them.* The inscription is much broken at this point, but we gather that the king attacked the foe with his

Fig. 25.—A Pharaoh carried in Triumph through the Streets of Thebes. (*After Lepsius.*)

spear, and captured at least one Asiatic, together with his chariot, horses, and accoutrements, the last consisting of a coat of mail, two bows, a quiver full of arrows, and a corselet.

During this campaign Amenhotpe entirely crushed the revolt, and brought back with him to Egypt seven of the revolted Syrian dynasts.

He went up to Thebes by river, and, as he drew near the city, these unfortunates were suspended alive, head downwards, from the prow of his vessel. Passing along the streets of his capital

Fig. 26.—The Pharaoh sacrificing Prisoners of War in the Presence of a Divinity.

(*After* Lepsius.)

in triumph (see Fig. 25), he proceeded to the temple of Amūn, where, by way of expressing his gratitude to the god for having given him the victory, he sacrificed with his own hand the seven

SOME GREAT KINGS IN TIME OF WAR 101

poor wretches in the god's presence (see Fig 26). Six of the bodies were hanged upon the walls of Thebes, but the seventh was sent to Napata, the capital of Nubia, to be hanged upon the walls of that city as a warning to the Sudanese of what would befall them if they dared rebel against the Egyptian king.

It is related that there was no one who could draw Amenhotpe II.'s bow, *because his strength was so much greater than that of any king who has ever existed*, and it is interesting to note that the bow was actually found in his tomb. Professor Breasted thinks that we have here the origin of the story told by Herodotus, how the Persian Cambyses was unable to draw the bow of the king of Ethiopia.

Just at the end of the Nineteenth Dynasty great movements were taking place among the *peoples of the sea*, as the Egyptians designated the inhabitants of the north-eastern Mediterranean lands and the Greek islands. Conspicuous among these peoples were the Peleset and the Thekel, the former eventually colonizing the Palestinian coast, and better known to us under the name of Philistines, while the latter were possibly a branch of the pre-Greek Sikeloi or Sicilians. Associated with the Peleset and Thekel were the Denyen (Danaoi), Sherden, Weshwesh, and Shekelesh. All these peoples were forcing their way south both by land and sea, probably being driven forward by the pressure of other migrant peoples in their rear. By the beginning of Ramesses III.'s reign the Peleset and their confederates had pushed their way down into northern Syria as far as the upper waters of the Orontes, and their ships were actually creeping up the mouths of the Nile and harrying the Delta ports and the fertile lands adjacent thereto.

The Libyans had invaded the western Delta in the reign of the Nineteenth Dynasty Pharaoh Merneptah, and had been thoroughly defeated. But during the period of anarchy that intervened between the death of that Pharaoh (about 1215 B.C.) and the accession of Ramesses III. (about 1198 B.C.), the Libyans plucked up courage again and started plundering and harrying north-western Egypt, just as they had done in the past before they felt the weight of the Pharaoh's hand. Growing bolder and bolder, they now, under their king Thermer, determined upon an invasion on the grand scale, with the intention of permanently occupying and settling down in Egyptian territory. To make

SOME GREAT KINGS IN TIME OF WAR 103

more certain of accomplishing their aim, they made common cause with the sea-rovers, some of whom joined their land forces. A great combined attack was made on Egypt both by land and from the sea, and Ramesses, who had been preparing for this onslaught, engaged them in battle near the fortress-town named (later, of course) *Usermarē'-Miamūn is Chastiser of the Libyans*. A joint land and naval action was fought, in which the Pharaoh displayed great personal valour. He is described as being *a youth like a gryphon . . . a bull ready for battle; his steeds were like hawks*. The Libyans are said to have been *slain in their places in heaps before his horses*, Ramesses being *like Mont* (the warrior-god) *. . . charging into hundreds of thousands, mighty in valour, stretching the bow, and shooting the arrows whithersoever he will*. The invading hordes were thus totally routed, twelve thousand being slain, and a thousand or more taken prisoner. The hostile fleet was destroyed, all the ships being sunk or captured.

The captives and a vast amount of booty were brought to the palace to be displayed before the king, who inspected them from the balcony, the nobles and courtiers standing below and acclaiming their victorious sovereign. A certain number of the prisoners were sacrificed by the king to Amūn, who had granted him the victory.

Security was thus restored to the western Delta, where there had been no security for years, and Ramesses boasted that a woman could now walk abroad as she pleased with her veil raised and suffer no molestation.

But the sea-rovers who had rendered naval and military assistance to the Libyans in the western Delta, were no more than the advanced guard of the mighty host pressing on into Syria. The Syrian dynasts were quite unable to resist the overwhelming flood of invaders—a concourse of nations on the march. All the Hittite country in northern Syria was overrun and the Hittite power in that region broken for ever. Still further south the kingdom of Amor was overwhelmed and devastated. Conjointly with their advance by land, these semi-barbarous hordes attacked by sea with their formidable fleets, ravaging the coast towns of western Cilicia and of the north Syrian littoral. Those they attacked seem to have been so stricken with terror that only a feeble resistance was put up.

Ramesses III. alone kept his head and, determining to defend his Empire, prepared for the coming onslaught with great energy. He fortified

DEIR EL-BAHRI.
General view of Queen Hatshepsut's temple at Thebes. (See pp. 128, 135, 162 foll.)

his Syrian frontier and having equipped a large and powerful fleet, distributed it among the various Syrian ports which were included in his dominion. He tells us in one of the long inscriptions still to be read on the walls of the temple of Medīnet Habu, how he *caused the harbour-mouths to be equipped like a strong wall with warships, galleys, and barges. They were manned completely from bow to stern with valiant warriors bearing their arms, soldiers of all the choicest of Egypt, being like lions roaring upon the mountain-tops. . . . I was the valiant Mont, stationed before them, that they might behold the graspings of my hands, (even the hands of) the king of Upper and Lower Egypt, Usermarēʿ, son of Rēʿ, Ramesses-Prince-of-On. I behaved as one who strides boldly forward, one who is conscious of his might, far-reaching of arm, who rescues his troops in the day of battle.*

Ramesses led his army in person into Syria and threw all his forces against the invaders. Exactly where the battle was fought is not known, but it is not likely to have taken place further north than Amor. The Medīnet Habu reliefs show us the Pharaoh's troops breaking through the enemy's lines and plundering their ox-carts, in which the barbarous northerners conveyed their women, children, and goods.

Having won this important land battle, the energetic king hurried to the sea-coast to take part in a naval action, which was fought between his navy and the fleet of the sea-rovers off one of the Phœnician ports. On each Egyptian vessel were stationed a number of the famous Egyptian archers, whose effective shooting decimated the forces on board the enemy ships before they could get alongside to board the Egyptian ships. Egyptian archers were also stationed on shore, and, under the king's personal direction, poured a hail of arrows on to the hostile fleet (see Fig. 27). The Egyptian ships then made for the ships of the enemy, which had now been thrown into confusion, and the troops proceeded to board them. The above-quoted inscription at Medīnet Habu thus describes the naval fight: *As for those who assembled before them* (the Egyptians) *on the sea, the full flame* (the Egyptian fleet) *confronted them at the harbour-mouth, and a wall of metal* (the Egyptian infantry) *enclosed them upon the shore. They were dragged, overturned, and cast down upon the beach; they were slain and heaped up from stern to bow of their vessels, everything was cast upon the water.* As for the

SOME GREAT KINGS IN TIME OF WAR 107

survivors who swam to shore, they were captured by the Egyptian soldiery on the beach.

Thus Ramesses, thanks to his foresight and his elaborate preparations, averted the disaster that threatened not only his Asiatic dominions, but ultimately indeed the eastern portion, if not the whole, of the Delta.

Fig. 27.—The Egyptian Naval Victory off the Coast of Phœnicia.
(*After Rossellini*, "*Monumenti Storici.*")

The two sea-fights described above are the earliest that history records for us, and, as has often happened since, they decided in either case the issue of a war.

But after a short respite the north-west frontier of Egypt was again threatened. The Libyans were invaded by the Meshwesh, a kindred people living to the west of them, and were forced by them into an alliance against Egypt. Meshersher, king of the Meshwesh, we are told, wished to settle with his subjects in the rich Delta lands. "*We will settle in Egypt.*" *So spake they with one accord, and they continuously entered the boundaries of Egypt.* At the end of the eleventh year of Ramesses III. these Meshwesh began seriously to invade the fertile plains of the western Delta, just as they had done in the days of Merneptaḥ, some forty to fifty years before, and proceeded to invest an Egyptian fortress called Ḥatsho', lying about eleven miles from the edge of the western desert. Ramesses engaged the enemy in battle outside this fortress, from the walls of which the Egyptian archers poured down a destructive hail of arrows. Caught between two fires, the invaders were routed and fled, and in their flight had to pass another fortress, where they proved an easy target for the archers stationed on the walls, and suffered further casualties. Ramesses drove the invaders right out of Egypt and back into the wilderness from which they had issued. Meshersher, king of the Meshwesh, and his father were captured, more than two thousand of the enemy were slain, and an equal number were made prisoners, a quarter of them being women. All these unfortunates were enslaved, men, women, and children alike, and were branded with the royal victor's name. Some were handed over to the captains of archers and turned into mercenary soldiers, and nearly a thousand were appointed to tend a herd of cattle belonging to the god Amūn.

This was the last war of the last of the great Egyptian War-Lords, who, if the official accounts are to be believed, himself figured conspicuously in the fighting. *The heart of his majesty was enraged, even as (that of) Baʿal in heaven; his whole body was endowed with strength and might. He betook himself . . . to lay hold of multitudes on his right hand and on his left, meeting their very selves, advancing like an arrow against them to slay them. His strength was mighty, like that of his father Amūn. Keper* (the father of the Meshwesh king) *came to salām . . . he laid down his arms together with his soldiers. He cried at the top of his voice to beseech his son's aid. Paralyzed (?) were his feet and his hands, and he stood stiff in his place. He* (i.e., the Pharaoh) *is the god who knew his* (Keper's) *inmost thoughts, even his majesty, who came down upon them* (the enemy) *like a mountain of granite. They were crushed, laid out, brought down to the ground, their blood was all about them like a flood, their bodies crushed on the spot, trampled upon. . . . Happy are his* (the Pharaoh's) *counsels, his plans have been achieved. He returns to his palace, his heart cheered. He is like a rapacious lion roaring, [from whom] the goats flee away—the king of Upper and Lower Egypt, Usermarē'-Miamūn, son of Rē', Ramesses-Prince-of-On. As for Egypt — their hearts rejoice at seeing his victories; they exult with one accord over the plight [of the foe].*

CHAPTER V

A FAMOUS QUEEN

THE three most remarkable of those very remarkable rulers who constitute the Eighteenth Egyptian Dynasty are undoubtedly D̠hutmōse III., Queen Ḥatshepsut, and Amenḥotpe IV. (otherwise known as Akhenaton, or, to be more correct, Ōkhnatōn). Some idea of D̠hutmōse's military prowess and of his strength of character can be gained from what has been said about him in the previous chapter, while the quotations from Amenḥotpe IV.'s famous hymn in Chapter VI. will reveal something of the charm of this extraordinary Pharaoh's personality and of the magnitude of his achievements in the field cf religion and thought. The aim of this chapter is briefly to set forth the life and works of Ḥatshepsut, perhaps the greatest woman that the Near East has ever produced, certainly the first woman-individualist in history—the first woman who attempted to show that woman can rival man in political life, aye and in some spheres even surpass him.

Dhutmōse I., who has appeared in Chapter IV. in the guise of a somewhat ferocious warrior, had two wives, the hereditary princess Ahmōse (a descendant through her mother of the great Nefretiri, the wife of king Ahmōse I.), and Mutnofret (a daughter of Amenhotpe I., but not an hereditary princess—that is to say, not of solar rank). By Queen Ahmōse Dhutmōse had a daughter, Hatshepsut, and by Mutnofret a son, who afterwards became Dhutmōse II. Hatshepsut was not only Dhutmōse I.'s elder child, but also the hereditary princess of the blood royal.

Towards the end of his reign, when Hatshepsut was aged about twenty-four, Dhutmōse I., apparently having fallen into a feeble condition of health, associated his daughter with him on the throne and proclaimed her his successor—nay, more, he actually had her crowned as ruler of Egypt during his lifetime; indeed, this association virtually amounted to the king's abdication. Such a proceeding as this was unheard of, for hitherto no woman had ever occupied the throne of the Pharaohs, except perhaps the shadowy Nitōkris, who is supposed to have reigned in her own right at the end of the Sixth Dynasty, a period, however, of anarchy and confusion.

DEIR EL-BAḤRI.
View towards Karnak from the so-called Birth-Hall in the temple of Hatshepsut.
(See p. 162.)

A FAMOUS QUEEN 113

So abnormal, indeed, was this enthronization of a woman, that all the reliefs executed during Hatshepsut's reign, that depict her as acting in this or that capacity, represent her in the habit of an ordinary Egyptian Pharaoh, and assign her a male figure. If it were not for feminine terminations and feminine pronouns in the accompanying inscriptions, no one would have any idea that what we have before us is a woman masquerading as a man. But despite the employment of feminine terminations and feminine pronouns, no attempt was made to create a feminine form of the word *nesut* ("king") or the compound *nesut-bīyet* ("king of Upper and Lower Egypt").

An inscription in the temple of Deir el-Bahri gives an account of the events leading up to the elevation of Hatshepsut to the throne, but puts it in a mythological rather than in an historical form. We are told that the princess grew up *greater than anything, more beautiful to behold than anything.* . . . *Her majesty grew up to be a beautiful maiden, fresh in her youth.* Apparently she went on several journeys with her royal father to Lower Egypt, and on every occasion all the gods and goddesses of the land *met her and showed her the good way. They came and brought her all the life and the good fortune that they bestow, and they encompassed her with their protection. One led the other, and they went round about her every day.* They said *"Welcome, welcome, daughter of Amūn! Behold thou thine administration in the land. Thou dost dispose it. Thou dost restore what is decayed in it. Thou makest thy monuments in our temples. Thou suppliest the food-tables of him who begat thee"* (i.e., Amunrēʽ). These divinities, having enumerated all her achievements and good works,—they speak as though she were accomplishing, or had already accomplished, them as actual ruler—then promise her the reward of length of days and happiness, assuring her at the same time that her *boundary will be as wide as heaven, extending to the limits of the twilight.*

We are told that on one of these journeys to the north she visited Heliopolis, the religious and political centre of Egypt in early times, its god, Rēʽ-Atum, the sun-god, as pointed out in Chapter III., being regarded as the first king of Egypt and the prototype of all Egyptian kings, while the Pharaoh on his part was considered to be the actual physical son of the sun-god—that god's embodiment on earth.

Every Egyptian Pharaoh, it would seem, in

A FAMOUS QUEEN 115

order to legitimize his rule, had to visit Rēʿ-Atum in his temple at Heliopolis, there to be recognized both as his offspring and as king. Accordingly Ḥatshepsut would have the world to understand that she, too, had received this recognition at the hands of the sun-god at Heliopolis, and a series of reliefs—unhappily much defaced—in the middle colonnade of the temple of Deir el-Baḥri depicts the queen's visit there.

We see four divinities leading Ḥatshepsut into the presence of Rēʿ-Atum, the sun-god, who welcomes her and promises her *the everlasting years of Horus*, and that *she shall lead the flat lands of Egypt*, and *make tributary the (foreign) hill-countries*, while she *lives like Rēʿ*.

The diadems of Upper and Lower Egypt are then brought to be placed on her head by Horus and Sēth, who represent respectively the Lower and Upper country (see Fig. 28), and who *establish the two mistresses* on her brow, and she assumes the diadems, namely the Upper and Lower Egyptian crowns, which are united for her.*

The actual ceremony of crowning over, the

* *I.e.*, the two crowns personified as the two tutelary goddesses of Lower and Upper Egypt, namely, Uto and Nekhbet.

queen's official names are proclaimed, and Thōth and Seshat, the god and goddess of writing and enumeration, are depicted recording these names in their books.

Fig. 28.—Horus and Sēth Crowning an Egyptian King.
(*After Wilkinson.*)

We next see the queen, arrayed in the royal robes and regalia, and invested with the insignia of her high office, being conducted into the presence

A FAMOUS QUEEN 117

of Amūn of Thebes, now identified with Rēʻ-Atum. This scene is, of course, a Theban innovation, designed to associate the *parvenu* god with the ancient traditional coronation ceremonies which had originated in Heliopolis. Amūn promises her *all health and all happiness, and the food which is in this land.* He tells her, moreover, that he has *given her all the flat lands (of Egypt) and all the (foreign) hill-countries. All that the sun's disk in heaven encompasseth are under thy control, while thou livest, even as I love thee.*

While Amūn thus addresses her, the "souls" of the prehistoric kings of Nekhen (the old capital of Upper Egypt), Buto (the old capital of Lower Egypt), and Heliopolis, who are depicted kneeling behind the queen, shout their greetings, and vie with the great gods in their assurances of long life, good fortune, health, and happiness.

Another relief in the temple of Deir el-Baḥri and the accompanying inscription, are definitely historical, and represent and describe the presentation of Ḥatshepsut to the great men of the country by her father, D̲hutmōse I. The old king, who is seated upon a canopied throne set upon a dais, lays his hands on his daughter, who turns round to face the assemblage in front of her (see Fig. 29). In

118 LUXOR AND ITS TEMPLES

the accompanying inscription we are told that the *majesty of this her father beheld her, how very godlike her form was, how pre-eminent her mind.* He noted how wisely she gave judgment, and was convinced that her royal worth was such that she must be given her due place, and accordingly be raised to the throne. *His majesty said unto her, "Come thou, thou glorious one, whom I have placed in my arms (i.e.,* associated with me on the throne), *that thou mayest see thy administration in the palace, that thou mayest take thy glorious position which is thy due, that thou mayest assume thy noble office, excellent in thy magic, mighty in thy strength; that thou mayest have power over the Two Lands, that thou mayest seize upon the rebellious, that thou mayest appear gloriously in the palace, thy brow being adorned with the double diadem, that thou mayest be happy as my*

Fig. 29.—Dhutmōse I. presenting Hatshepsut to the Great Men of Egypt.

(*After* Naville, "*Deir el-Bahari.*")

heir who is born to me, O daughter of the White Crown,* beloved of Uto."†

Dhutmōse I. accordingly gave instructions that all the nobles, high officials, and notables among the people were to be summoned into his presence, *in order to issue to them a command, while my majesty puts the majesty of this my daughter in his arms in his palace of the residence.*

There then *took place a sitting of the king himself* in a certain pillared hall, *while these people* (the notables and other great personages) *lay prostrate in the Court. His majesty said in their presence: " This my daughter Hatshepsut, I appoint her to be my substitute. Yea, she is my successor. She it is who shall sit on my wondrous throne. She shall give command to the people in all places of the palace. She it is who shall lead you, and ye shall hearken to her word. . . . He who praises her shall live, but he who saith aught evil, blaspheming her majesty, he shall die.*"

This utterance of the king was received with an outburst of loyal enthusiasm. We are told that those who had been summoned to hear the proclamation *kissed the ground at his* (the king's) *feet* . . .

* The crown of Upper Egypt, and equated with Nekhbet see above, p. 115, note.
† See *ibid.*

and went out rejoicing. They danced, they shouted for joy. The sounds of rejoicing were heard everywhere, and resounded through *all the rooms of the royal residence.* The soldiers and the crowds assembled outside the palace took up the cry, and *they published, they published, the name of her majesty as king,—albeit her majesty was still but a youth—for the great gods inclined their hearts to his daughter Makerē', and they knew her to be the daughter of a god.* The crowds kept on shouting : *Anyone who loves her in his heart, who praises her every day . . . he will flourish more than anything. Anyone who speaks evil against the name of her majesty, God will straightway ordain his death. Lo, it is the gods who encompass her with protection every day.*

The majesty of this her father, we are informed, *heard that all the people proclaimed the name of this his daughter as king—albeit her majesty was still a youth—and the heart of his majesty was glad more than anything.* He thereupon proceeded to make all the arrangements for the coronation, which he fixed for New Year's Day, for *he knew that a coronation on New Year's Day is auspicious as the beginning of peaceful years, and of her celebrating millions of many jubilees.*

XVII.

A FAMOUS QUEEN

The great day in Hatshepsut's life came at last— *the first day of the season of Inundation, New Year's Day, the beginning of peaceful years, the day of the Coronation of the King of Upper and Lower Egypt, (the day) of the Union of the Two Lands, the Procession round the Walls, the Festival of the Diadem.*

It would appear that the coronation ceremonies, the most important of which are schematically depicted, no doubt in the order of their enactment, on the north wall of the middle colonnade of the temple of Deir el-Bahri, were performed in the palace precincts, a number of special chapels being erected for the occasion. The first ceremony was the lustral washing of the Pharaoh-designate, who had to be made absolutely free of all possible earthly contamination before the two diadems could be placed on his head; these, as has already been pointed out on p. 115, being regarded by the Egyptians as the actual embodiments of the goddesses Nekhbet and Uto, and their curatorship reckoned a priestly office. Accordingly a priest, called the Pillar of his Mother, is seen leading Hatshepsut into one of the above-mentioned chapels, which was designated the Great House, this being the name of the sanctuary of Hierakonpolis, the pre-dynastic capital of Upper Egypt.

In this chapel a priest, impersonating Yaḥes, the god of the West, sprinkled the queen with holy water, which not only was thought to purify her, but to endow her with *life, good fortune, stability, health, and happiness*, whereby she would be able to *celebrate very many jubilees like Rē' for ever.*

After this preliminary purification, a priest impersonating the god Horus conducted Ḥatshepsut into another room, which was identified with the sanctuary of Buto, the pre-dynastic capital of Lower Egypt, where he and another priest who impersonated Sēth—the two, as we have seen, respectively representing the northern and southern halves of the realm—crowned her with the white crown of Upper Egypt.

Ḥatshepsut then came forth from the chapel, preceded by four officiants carrying each a sacred standard, and showed herself to the people in front of the palace. This proceeding, which was designated *the Union of the Two Lands, the Procession round the Walls, going round on the Eastern Side*, commemorated the triumphal procession of Menes, the first king of the First Dynasty, round the walls of Memphis, in celebration of his conquest of Lower Egypt, the event which had brought about *the Union of the Two Lands.* It is here to be

A FAMOUS QUEEN 123

noted that the words " Procession round the walls " are the equivalent of " Procession round Memphis," for the White Walls, or simply the Walls, was the old name of that city,—the great white fortification

Fig. 30.—Hatshepsut assuming the Red Crown of Lower Egypt and then leaving the Chapel.
(*After* Naville.)

walls, which had been erected by Menes himself, being its characteristic feature.

After this commemorative procession, Hatshepsut again entered the chapel in which she had been crowned with the white crown, in order that she might also be crowned with the red crown of Lower

Egypt. Again she issued from the chapel, preceded this time by two standard-bearers (see Fig. 30), and paraded in front of the palace, and with this procession the coronation ceremonial seems to have terminated.

The Deir el-Baḥri reliefs give only a bare outline of what we have reason to believe was a very lengthy and elaborate rite. They do not, for example, depict what was undoubtedly one of many other coronation ceremonies—namely, the letting fly of four birds, usually geese, to carry the news to the four quarters of heaven that *Horus son of Isis and Osiris has assumed the great crown of Upper and Lower Egypt, that king N. has received the great crown of Upper and Lower Egypt* (see below, p. 181, and Fig. 48). A document containing this information was sometimes tied round the neck of each bird (see Fig. 31).

During the performance of every ritual act certain prescribed formulæ were recited, and these sometimes, it would seem, took the form of a dialogue between the king and the leading priestly officiants, in which the former was instructed by the latter as to what his duties would be in his capacity of son of the sun-god and the earthly embodiment of that divinity. The gist of one of these didactic discourses is perhaps preserved to us by a Latin writer called Nigidius Figulus, who tells us that before the Pharaoh was crowned he was straitly charged not to tamper with the 365-days Calendar (apparently first instituted in Heliopolis in the year 4241 B.C.), being bound by an oath never

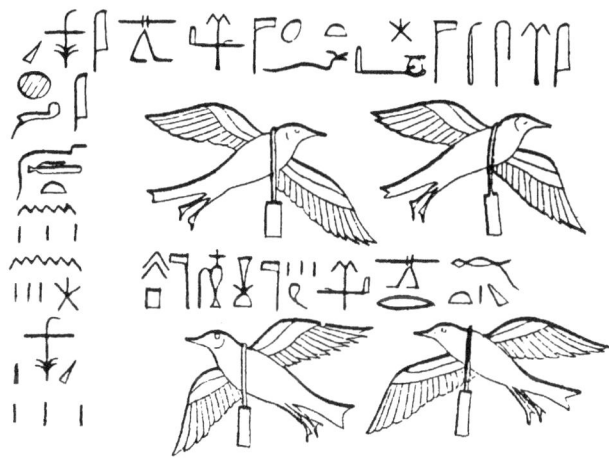

Fig. 31.—Carrier-Birds with Messages attached to their Necks.
(*After Lepsius.*)

to intercalate a month or even a day, nor alter the date of a festival, but perpetuate the 365 days as instituted by the ancients.

Dhutmōse I. must have realized the abnormality of the situation he had created by making Hatshepsut Pharaoh, for not long before he died —no doubt to make her position more secure—he married her to his son, her half-brother, Dhutmōse II., who came to the throne as nominal Pharaoh when death finally overtook the sick king.

On the earlier monuments of this joint reign Hatshepsut is depicted as occupying the ordinary position of an Egyptian queen, assisting the king at the celebration of the temple liturgy in the capacity of high-priestess, and otherwise playing a quite subordinate *rôle*. But this was all outward seeming, and did not long prevail even in representations so stereotyped as Egyptian temple reliefs. Ere long such reliefs began to depict her as on an equal footing with her brother-husband, and when he died, aged about thirty—he was a weakling, physically, and perhaps also intellectually—Hatshepsut was left sole legitimate ruler at the age of about thirty-seven, with no one to challenge her right except a small nephew of about ten years of age, also named Dhutmōse (the son of her husband by a secondary wife of non-solar rank), who was afterwards known to fame as Dhutmōse III., and whom immediately, or not long, after his father's death she associated with herself on the throne.

Hatshepsut must have possessed unusual ability and been gifted with great determination and strength of character. For a woman to have been

A FAMOUS QUEEN

for thirty years or more the acting head of an oriental military monarchy was surely an amazing achievement. She reminds one in some ways of our own Elizabeth, and like her, in addition to being strong-minded, had the good fortune to possess, or discrimination to choose, capable and shrewd advisers.

During the last ten years of Hatshepsut's reign, when he had fully attained manhood, Dhutmōse III. must have longed for some opportunity to display his military and administrative talents; but strong man though he later proved himself to be, he was no match for his aunt, who seems to have allowed him no authority whatever. It was not till her death that his genius as a general blazed forth, when, accompanied by his legions, he thundered through Syria in seventeen victorious campaigns. How he must have chafed at petticoat government! For while he lusted for the battle, he was condemned by his elderly and tyrannical relative to content himself with such paltry functions as those of a thurifer in a religious procession. Imagine Napoleon as an acolyte!

Owing to the military prowess of her immediate predecessors, Hatshepsut's reign was a period of peace, and she was thus able to occupy herself in developing the vast and newly acquired resources of her Empire. She devoted herself to architectural works—restoring those temples that had lain in ruin since the Hyksōs occupation—and to commercial enterprise and exploration.

Ḥatshepsut's perhaps most famous achievement was the expedition she fitted out and despatched to the land of Punt, a country supposed to have been situated some way down the Red Sea in the region now called Somaliland, or perhaps even further south than that. In her temple at Deir el-Baḥri, on the southern wall of the middle colonnade, she tells us all about this venture in a series of very beautiful and detailed reliefs accompanied by explanatory and often most interesting inscriptions.

We are told that the queen was one day *making supplication at the steps* (i.e., the steps leading up to the enthroned image) *of the lord of gods*, when *a command was heard (issuing) from the Great Place* (the part of the sanctuary where the shrine stood), *an oracle of the god himself, that the ways to Punt should be searched out, that the roads to the myrrh-terraces (*i.e., the hill-sides on which the myrrh-trees grew) *should be opened up, that an expedition should be led over water and over land, in order to fetch the marvels from God's-Land for this*

RAMESSEUM.

A FAMOUS QUEEN

god who fashioned her (Ḥatshepsut's) *beauties. It was done,* the inscription goes on to say, *according to all that the majesty of this august god commanded,* the queen straightway equipping and despatching a fleet of five ships. This fleet, so Professor Breasted suggests, sailed down the Nile from Thebes, and then passed along a canal, which, it is supposed, ran at that time through the Wādy Ṭūmīlāt and connected the river with the Red Sea.

Fig. 32.—Perehu and his Fat Wife.
(*After Naville.*)

In due course the fleet arrived safely at Punt, where the Egyptians were received in the most friendly fashion by Perehu, the Puntite chief, and his wife (see Fig. 32). The inhabitants of Punt were not negroes but Hamites, and they accordingly possessed, as the Deir el-Baḥri reliefs show, much the same facial features and other physical characteristics as the Egyptians. Perehu's right leg, it will be observed, is covered from ankle to knee with metal or ivory rings. His wife is an extraordinary-looking creature, and it has been suggested that she suffered from elephantiasis. As a matter of fact, however, the sculptor has merely represented for us one of those enormously fat women, a taste for whom is widespread among the peoples of Africa, and is not unknown even in modern Egypt!

It was so long a time since any Egyptians had been seen in Punt that the natives are represented in the Egyptian narrative of events as crying out: *Why have ye come hither unto this land which people knew not? Did ye come down upon the ways of heaven? Did ye voyage over water, over land?* They then speak flatteringly of the Pharaoh, and express a desire to pay their homage to him in Egypt. *The king of Egypt, is there not a way unto his majesty, that we may live on the breath which he gives?*

The preliminary interchange of compliments over, the Egyptian explorers settled down to the business on which they had come—namely, the acquiring of the valuable raw materials and other commodities produced by this outlandish country, in return for the manufactured goods they had

A FAMOUS QUEEN 131

brought with them. *A tent was erected,* we read, *for the king's envoy and his troops in the myrrh-terraces of Punt beside the great green ocean, in order to receive the chieftains of this land. There was offered to them* (the native chiefs) *bread, beer,*

Fig. 33.—The "King's Envoy" receiving the Puntites.
(*After Mariette, "Deir el-Bahari."*)

wine, meat, and fruits, every thing which is (produced) in Egypt, according to what had been ordered at the Court.

The reliefs show us the *king's envoy* standing before the tent and receiving the Puntites, who are bringing the products of their country to exchange them for some of those bead-necklaces, hatchets, daggers, and the like, which have been temptingly laid out before them (see Fig. 33). Behind the Puntites is depicted the village or settlement from which they have issued with their wares. It was evidently a thickly-wooded country, and the huts of the natives peep out from amid various kinds of trees. These huts are of the typically African beehive variety, but they are erected on piles, and access to each was gained by a ladder. At the bottom of the relief is a strip of water full of fish, showing that the settlement was situated close to the seashore or on the edge of some creek (see Fig. 34). It has been suggested that the erection of huts on piles denotes a swampy country, but we are distinctly told that the myrrh-trees grew on *terraces*—that is, on the sides of hills —and the tent mentioned above, and shown in Fig. 34, was erected *in the myrrh-terraces*. Mr. H. Weld-Blundell has suggested to me that the huts are built on piles as a protection against white ants, with which Somaliland is infested. There are just one or two kinds of wood, of which the piles would have been made, that these pests will not devour.

Evidently the hatchets, beads, and other gawds caught the fancy of the simple Puntites, for the

A FAMOUS QUEEN

Egyptians soon began to load their vessels with *the marvels of the country of Punt.* Gangways were run out, and up them filed the porters in a seemingly endless procession, bearing *all the goodly fragrant woods of To-Nūter,** *heaps of myrrh-resin, together with living incense-trees* (which were to be transplanted in Egypt), *ebony, ivory,*

Fig. 34.— Part of a Puntite Village.
(*After Mariette.*)

gold, cinnamon-wood, . . . *incense, eye-cosmetic, baboons, monkeys, dogs, skins of Upper Egyptian panthers* (see Fig. 35). Included in the cargo were a number of the natives themselves and their children. *Never, we are told, was the like of this brought for any king that there had been since primæval time.*

* = " God's-Land "; also used as a designation of the Lebanon country (see above, p. 74).

The fleet had a fair return voyage without mishap, and finally moored again at the Theban docks, where the ships were unloaded. A great procession was formed, led by the commander of the expedition, and all the strange products of that far-off land were paraded through the streets of the capital to the palace, where they were formally

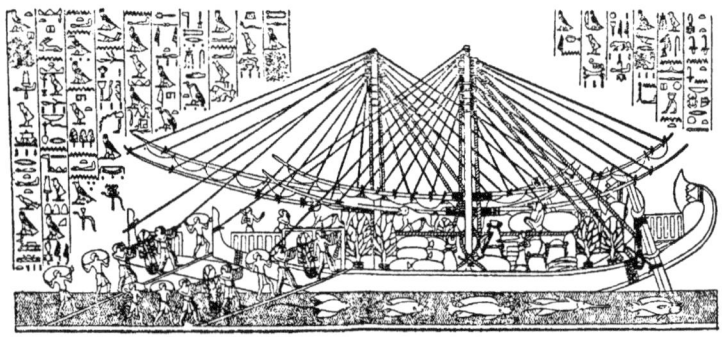

Fig. 35.—Loading the Egyptian Vessels with the Produce of Punt.
(*After Breasted*, " *History of Egypt.*")

presented to the queen. In this procession walked a number of the natives of Punt themselves, and it must have been a wonderful spectacle for the Thebans, who had never before witnessed such a show.

Hatshepsut made over to Amūn, who had commanded the expedition to be despatched, his share of the spoils. It is most interesting to learn that the live incense-trees were exported especially for

A FAMOUS QUEEN

him. Deir el-Baḥri temple is built in three terraces, one above the other (see below, p. 162), and on these terraces the trees were planted. Thus an attempt was made to reproduce the effect of the natural terraces or hill-slopes of the country from whence the trees had been brought. *I made for him*, says Ḥatshepsut, *a Punt in his garden, according to what he commanded me, at Thebes. It is large enough for him to walk about in.*

Ḥatshepsut's reign, brilliant though it was, seems to have led to the weakening of the Egyptian military position in Syria and northern Palestine. The queen and her ministers so devoted themselves to architectural undertakings, exploration, and other peaceful pursuits,—forgetting that it is the strong man armed who keeps his house—that by the end of her reign the Egyptians' hold on their Asiatic dominion was in jeopardy. Her death came none too soon, and it gave Dhutmōse the opportunity for which he had been longing during the tedious years of his subordination.

CHAPTER VI

POEMS, SONGS, AND ROMANCES

THE Imperial Age is no less noteworthy for its literary than for its military and artistic achievements; indeed, many of the poems and other compositions then produced are quite equal, if not superior, to the best work of the preceding period, the so-called Middle Kingdom, which is generally regarded as the Classical Period of Egyptian literature. Certain of the triumphant songs composed in honour of the great Emperors' acts of prowess in war are distinguished by really fine writing, a good example of such being the Victory Hymn of Ḏhutmōse III., in which the poet represents the god Amūn as thus addressing the Pharaoh:

I have come that I may cause thee to tread down the princes of Palestine,
That I may spread them out under thy feet throughout their countries;
That I may cause them to behold thy majesty as a lord of radiance,
While thou shinest in their faces in my similitude.

HYPOSTYLE HALL, RAMESSEUM.
Looking diagonally across to S.E. corner.

I *have come that I may cause thee to tread down those who
   are in Asia,*
To smite the heads of the Syrians of Retenu ;
*That I may cause them to behold thy majesty equipped
   with thine accoutrements,*
When thou layest hold on the weapons of war in the chariot.

I *have come that I may cause thee to tread down the eastern
   land,*
To trample on those who are in the regions of To-Nūter ;*
*That I may cause them to behold thy majesty as the star
   Seshed,†*
When it scatters its flame in fire, when it gives forth its dew.

I *have come that I may cause thee to tread down the
   western land,*
Crete and Cyprus (?) are in terror of thee ;
*That I may cause them to behold thy majesty as a young
   bull,*
Firm of heart, with horns ready, irresistible.

I *have come that I may cause thee to tread down them that
   are in their marshes,*
The lands of Meten‡ tremble for fear of thee ;
That I may cause them to behold thy majesty as a crocodile,
Lord of terror in the water, unapproachable.

I *have come that I may cause thee to tread down them that
   are in the islands,*
*They that are in the midst of the great green sea hear thy
   battle-cry :*

---

* See above, p. 133, note.
† Name of a star or constellation.   ‡ Unidentified.

*That I may cause them to behold thy majesty as the
    Avenger,**
Who appeared gloriously upon the back of his slain foe.

I have come that I may cause thee to tread down the Libyans,
The Uthentyu† are subject to the might of thy prowess ;
*That I may cause them to behold thy majesty as a fierce-
    eyed lion,*
While thou makest them as corpses throughout their valley.

*I have come that I may cause thee to tread down the utter-
    most ends of the lands,*
What the great Encircler (the Ocean) *encircleth are held
    in thy grasp ;*
*That I may cause them to behold thy majesty as a lord of
    the wing* (*i.e.*, a hawk),
Who seizeth upon what he seeth, according as he desireth.

*I have come that I may cause thee to tread down those who
    are in the country nigh at hand,*
To bind the sand-dwellers as living captives ;
*That I may cause them to behold thee as a jackal of Upper
    Egypt,*
A master of speed, a runner, traversing the Two Lands.

*I have come that I may cause thee to tread down the nomads
    of Nubia,*
As far as Shat‡ all is in thy grasp ;

---

       * *I.e.*, Horus, the avenger of Osiris.
       † Unknown people.
       ‡ Unknown region in Nubia.

POEMS, SONGS, AND ROMANCES 139

That I may cause them to behold thy majesty as thy two brethren,*
Whose hands I have joined for thee in victory.

The following is part of King Merneptah's song of triumph, and it is a particularly interesting passage, as it contains the earliest mention of Israel that we know of, and the only mention of that people in an Egyptian text:

The princes lie prone and say Salām.
There is not one who lifts up his head among the Nine Bows.†
Libya is wasted,
The Hittite land is pacified,
Canaan is captured with every evil,
Askalon is carried away,
Gezer is seized upon.
Yenoam is made as nothing,
Israel is desolated, her seed is not,
Palestine has become a widow for Timuris.‡
All lands are united in peace,
Everyone that is turbulent,—
He is bound by the King of
Upper and Lower Egypt Binerēʿ-Mıamūn,
Son of Rēʿ, Merneptah-Ḥetpḥermēʿet.

---

* Horus and Sēth, the representative gods of Lower and Upper Egypt.
† Ancient designation for the hostile neighbours of Egypt.
‡ Greek rendering of Egyptian $T'_{,-}mry$ = Egypt.

In the hymn celebrating the heroism of Ramesses II. when he fought against the Hittites, we get the nearest approach in all Egyptian literature to epic poetry.* We are told how the foe covered the hills like grasshoppers, and all the subsequent events, the rout of a division of the Egyptian army (the division of Rē'), their rush for safety to Ramesses' camp, the panic that seized on all the troops round about the Pharaoh,—all are made to lead up to the supreme moment when Ramesses found himself alone in the midst of the foe:

When his majesty looked behind him,
He marked that two thousand five hundred chariots encircled him in his outward way. . . .
No chief is with me,
No charioteer,
No officer of foot-soldiery,
Nor of chariotry.
My foot-soldiery and my chariotry have left me for a prey unto them (the enemy);
None of them stands fast in order to fight with them.

The poet represents him as calling on his father Amūn for aid:

* For a full account of the battle see Breasted, "Ancient Records of Egypt," Chicago, 1906, iii., pp. 123-162; "A History of Egypt," London, 1906, pp. 425-435.

What is it, then, my father Amūn?
Has a father indeed forgotten his son?
Have I done aught without thee?
If I went or stood still, was it not at thy command?
Never have I disregarded the decrees which thou hast
  ordained.
How great is the great lord of Thebes!
Too great for the stranger-peoples to be able to approach
  him.
What are these Asiatics to thee, O Amūn,
Wretches who know nought of God?

Ramesses, having first enumerated all the gifts he has bestowed on Amūn, draws the god's attention to his own desperate need, and asserts that he trusts in him alone:

Have I not made for thee very many monuments,
And filled thy temple with my captives?
I have built for thee my temple of millions of years,
And given thee my goods for (thy) possession.
All lands together do I present unto thee,
In order to furnish thine offering with victuals.
I cause to be offered to thee tens of thousands of oxen,
With all sweet-smelling plants.
No good thing leave I undone in thy temple.
I build for thee pylons and myself erect their flag-staffs.
I bring for thee obelisks from Elephantine,
And I it is that bring the stones.
I cause galleys to voyage for thee upon the sea,
In order to fetch for thee the tribute of the lands.
Mischief shall befall him who thwarts thy purposes,
But well he fares who understands (?) thee.

One should work for thee with a loving heart.
I call on thee, my father Amūn.
I am in the midst of strangers, whom I know not.
All lands have joined themselves together against me,
And I am all alone and none other is with me.
My soldiers have forsaken me,
Not one among my chariotry has looked round for me.
If I cry to them, not one of them hearkens.
But I call, and I see that Amūn is worth more to me than
  millions of foot-soldiers,
More than hundreds of thousands of chariots. . . .
The deeds of many men are nothing;
Amūn is worth more than they.
I have come hither by the decree of thy mouth, O Amūn,
And from thy decree have I not swerved.

Ramesses realizes that though he is far from the Thebaid, yet Amūn has heard, and is ready at hand to help him, enabling him to perform prodigies of valour:

I pray at the limits of the lands, yet my voice reaches unto
  Hermonthis.
Am n hears me and comes, when I cry to him.
He stretches out his hand to me, and I rejoice,
He calls out behind me: " Forward, forward! I am with
  thee, I thy father.
My hand is with thee and I am of more avail than a
  hundred-thousand men,
I, the lord of victory, who love strength."
I have found my courage again, my heart swells for joy,
What I am fain to do comes to pass.

I am as Mont, I shoot on the right hand and fight on the
    left,
I am in their presence as Ba'al in his time,
I see that the two thousand five hundred chariots, in whose
    midst I was,
Lie hewn in pieces before my steeds.
Not one of them has found his hand to fight.
Their hearts have become faint in their bodies for fear,
Their arms are all become powerless,
They are unable to shoot,
And have not the heart to take their lances.

I cause them to plunge into the water, as plunge the
    crocodiles.
They stumble one over the other, and I slay of them whom I
    will.
Not one of them looks back and there is none who turns
    round.
Whosoever of them falleth lifts not up himself again.

The Egyptian poet, as Professor Breasted has pointed out, has a real appreciation of the value of dramatic contrast. He throws the personal valour of the Pharaoh into high relief by setting against it the dismay of his charioteer, whose heart fails him when he realizes the utter loneliness of his own and his royal master's position :

But when, Menna, my charioteer, saw that a great multi-
    tude of chariots compassed me round about,
He became faint and his heart failed him, and very great
    fear entered into his body.

Then said he to his majesty: " *My good lord, valiant prince,*
  great protector of Egypt in the day of battle,
We stand alone in the midst of the foe.
Behold, our soldiers and our chariotry abandon us.
Wherefore wilt thou stay until they bereave (*us of breath*) *?*
Let us remain unscathed! Save us, O Ramesses!"

Then said his majesty to his charioteer:
" *Steady, steady thy heart, my charioteer!*
I am going in among them even as a hawk strikes.
I slay, hew in pieces, and throw to the ground.
What thinkest thou of these cowards?
My face grows not pale for millions of them!"

Ramesses, the poet goes on to tell us, dashed in among the foe with such fury that his discomforted troops took courage. They rushed in after him and turned a defeat into a victory, driving the Hittites into the river Orontes.

On a wall of the Ramesseum (see below, pp. 171 foll.) is a relief depicting the events described in the poem. We see the routed enemy plunging into the river and swimming across or struggling in the water, while some of them are being pulled to land by their friends on the opposite bank. A humorous touch is afforded by a group of figures comprising the king of Aleppo (see Fig. 36). This potentate, who was in league with the Hittites, has just been dragged out of the river,

MEDÎNET HABU.
Second colonnaded court in the funerary temple of Ramesses III.

and his rescuers are holding him upside down so that he may disgorge all the water that he has swallowed! Above the group is written: *The wretched chief of Aleppo turned upside down by his soldiers, after his majesty hurled him into the water.*

Fig. 36.—The King of Aleppo held upside-down by his Rescuers.
(*After Breasted.*)

After making all due allowance for the poet's imagination, and for his desire to please his royal patron, it cannot be doubted that Ramesses displayed great courage and presence of mind in this crisis. There is something, too, of the spirit of the heroes of Greek epic in the Pharaoh's vow that his gallant steeds, *Victory-in-Thebes* and *Mut-is-content*, which had borne him safely through the thick of the fray, should ever after be fed daily in his presence.

The following poem was written in celebration of the coronation of Ramesses IV. No doubt similar verses were sung or recited on the occasion of the coronation of Hatshepsut (see above, pp. 121 foll).

What a happy day! Heaven and earth rejoice, for thou art the great lord of Egypt.
Those who had fled have returned again to their towns, and those who were hidden have again come forth.
Those who hungered are satisfied and happy, and those who thirsted are drunken.
Those who were naked are clad in fine linen, and he who was dirty is full of joy.
Those who were at strife in this land are reconciled.
High Niles have come from their sources that they may refresh the hearts of men.
Widows, their houses stand open and they suffer the travellers to enter.
The maidens rejoice and repeat their songs of gladness.
They are arrayed in ornaments and they say:
". . . he creates generation on generation.
Thou ruler, thou wilt endure for ever."

The ships rejoice on the deep. . . .
They come to land with wind or oars.
They are satisfied . . . when it is said:

POEMS, SONGS, AND ROMANCES 147

" *The King Ḥekmē'etrē'-Miamūn again wears the crown,
The son of Rē', Ramesses, has received the office of his
 father.*"
All lands say to him:
" *Beautiful is Horus* (i.e., the king) *on the throne of
 Amūn who sends him forth,
(Amūn) the protector of the sovereign, who presents (unto
 him) every land.*

A certain number of folk-tales survive from the Imperial Age, of which the best known is the so-called "Tale of the Two Brothers." Two brothers, Anūp and Bata, lived happily together tilling their land. But, alas! one day Bata, the younger and unmarried brother, was tempted by Anūp's wife, who had for long been in love with him. Bata, like Joseph of Hebrew fame, resisted the woman's blandishments, but she, like Mistress Potiphar, putting on the outraged wife, accused the innocent youth to her husband, who thereupon tried to slay him. Bata, poor lad, accordingly fled from his home with his hot-headed assailant close on his heels brandishing a knife. In his distress he appealed to the sun-god Re'-Ḥarakhte, who straightway caused a broad stream of water, teeming with crocodiles, to spring up between the pursuer and the pursued. The tale then merges into a series of marvellous happenings, and, though full of interest to the student of folklore, loses much of the simple idyllic charm of the beginning.

Another popular tale of this period is the "Story of the Doomed Prince." A son was at last born to a childless king. The seven Hathors, or Fates, who came to decree his destiny, foretold that he would die through a snake, a crocodile, or a dog. When the child grew up, he set out, like the princes in our stories, to seek his fortune, accompanied by his faithful hound. He came at length to the far-off land of Mitanni, where there was a princess whose father had shut her up in a high tower perched on the top of a hill. Whoever succeeded in climbing up the sheer walls of the castle, and reached the window of the room in which the princess was confined, was to be proclaimed her husband.

Our hero, of course, performed this feat, which other wooers had been essaying for years. The princess in return saved his life from a snake. But alas! the rest of the story is lost, and so we do not know whether she also rescued him from the crocodile and the dog. It would be interesting to know how the ancient story-teller solved the problem. Did the prince, by his wife's aid, avoid his doom altogether, or did he somehow fall a victim to his own dog? Perhaps complete versions of this and other similar stories will be found in the tomb of Tut'enkhamūn!

Now for some examples of love-songs, such as the Egyptian peasants still sing:

> *I will lay me down in my chamber,*
> *For I am sick of the wrong (done me).*
> *My neighbours will come in to see me.*
> *Should my beloved come with them,*
> *She would put to shame the physicians,*
> *For she knoweth my sickness.*

A love-sick maiden sings:

It is the voice of the swallow that speaketh;
It saith: " The earth is bright, whither goest thou?"
Ah! no, O bird! Thou makest me to sicken.
I have found my lover in his bed and my heart rejoiceth.
He saith to me: " I will not betake me far from thee;
My hand abideth in thy hand.
I walk to and fro and am together with thee in every pleasant place."
He maketh me the chief of the maidens and causeth not my heart to be sick.

In an unfortunately ill-preserved and rather unintelligible song a young man exclaims:

Ah! would I were her negress who is her handmaid,
Then would I behold the colour of all her limbs. . . .
Ah! would I were her signet ring, which is fastened on her finger. . . .

Another song is supposed to be sung by a girl making a wreath of flowers. As she plies her task she cries:

> *Blush roses are in it—one blushes before thee.*
> *I am thy first sister.*
> *I am for thee as the garden,*
> *Which I have planted with flowers,*
> *And all manner of sweet-smelling herbs.*
> *Fair is the water-channel therein,*
> *Which thy hand hath digged,*
> *When the north wind blows cool,*
> *The beauteous place where I walk about,*
> *With thy hand resting in mine,*
> *And my heart satiated with delight,*
> *Because we walk together.*
> *It is intoxication for me to hear thy voice,*
> *And I live because I hear it.*
> *Whenever I see thee,*
> *It is better for me than food and drink.*

This is a charming little poem about the sycamore tree—personified as a maiden—in the shadow of which the lovers sit:

> *The little sycamore, which she* (the beloved) *hath planted with her hand,*
> *Which moves her mouth to speak.*
> *The whispering of her leaves is sweet as refined honey.*
> *How charming are her pretty twigs. . . .*
> *She is laden with fruits,*
> *Which are red as jasper.*

Her foliage is like unto malachite and is . . . as glass.
Her wood is the colour of felspar.
She draws (to herself) those who are not (already) under her,
Her shadow is (so) cool.

She slips a letter into the hand of a little maid,
The daughter of her chief gardener,
And makes her run to the beloved.
" Come and pass the time in the midst of thy maiden.*
The garden is in full bloom:
There are bowers and shelters there for thee.
My gardeners are glad and rejoice when they see thee.
Send thy slaves ahead of thee,
Supplied with their utensils,
To be sure, one is already drunken when one hastens to thee,
Before one has yet drunk.
But the servants come from thee with their vessels,
And bring beer of every kind and all manner of bread,
And many flowers of yesterday and to-day,
And all manner of refreshing fruit.
Come and spend a happy day,
Yea, to-morrow and the day after,
Three whole days in my shadow!"

Her (the beloved's) *lover sits on her right hand.*
She maketh him drunken and listens to all that he saith. . . .
But I (the tree) *am silent and tell nought of what* I *see.*
I *will say no word.*

There are many more songs such as these preserved to us, but the space available does not allow

* *I.e.,* beneath the boughs of the tree personified as a girl.

more examples to be cited here. Moreover, as yet a whole field of literature has not been touched— the religious poetry of the Imperial Age. Much of this poetry is inspired with the conception of God as a beneficent being who loves all his creatures, and who is in close personal relationship with man, if he will but realize it—a sentiment that is not apparent to anything like the same extent in the literature of the earlier periods.

In a hymn to Amunrē', preserved in Cairo, that divinity is said to be:

He who created herbs for the cattle,
And the fruit tree for men;
Who maketh that whereon live the fishes in the stream,
And the birds who (dwell) in the firmament;
He who giveth breath to that which is in the egg,
And maketh to live the son of the worm;
He who maketh that whereon the gnats live,
The worms and the flies likewise;
He who maketh what the mice in their holes need,
And sustaineth the birds on all the trees.

In another hymn of the same period Amūn appears in the guise of the good herdsman:

Amūn, thou herdsman, who early seest after the cows,
Who leadest the patient to the pasture.
The herdsman drives the cows to the pasture;
O Amūn, so thou drivest the patient to (their) bread.
For Amūn is a herdsman, a herdsman who is not idle.

XXII.

Amūn is also addressed as—

Thou pilot, who knowest the water!
Amūn, thou rudder . . .
Thou experienced one, who knowest the shoals,
Who art longed after by him who is on the water!
Amūn is present when one longs after him upon the water.

There is a distinct sense of personal relationship with the god in the concluding lines of the hymn:

O Amūn, I love thee and I trust in thee. . . .
Thou wilt deliver me from the mouth of man
In the day wherein he speaks lies. . . .
I follow not the care in my heart.
What Amūn hath said cometh to pass.

It is to Amūn again that the following verses represent a poor and defenceless claimant in the law-courts as appealing:

Amūn, lend thine ear to one who stands alone in the court
  of justice!
The tribunal oppresseth him!
" Silver and gold for the scribe!
Clothes for the attendants!"
But it is found that Amūn changeth himself into the vizier,
Whereby he maketh the poor man to overcome.
So it is found that the poor man is justified,
And the poor man passeth by the rich.

The most beautiful in some respects of all extant Egyptian religious poems is the hymn to Thōth in one of the British Museum papyri, that known as *Sallier Papyrus No.* 1. Thōth was the god of writing and recording, and he it was who recorded in his book the result of the weighing of the heart at the judgment of the dead before Osiris. He was also the advocate who had successfully pleaded the cause of Osiris against Sēth at the great trial held before Rēʻ, the sun-god, in Heliopolis. Accordingly, in the Imperial Age, when, by a process of democratization, all dead Egyptians were identified with Osiris, men and women alike looked to Thōth to plead their cause and obtain a favourable verdict for them at the great Assize.

The hymn in question is as follows:

O Thōth, place me in Hermopolis,*
In thy city, where life is pleasant.
Thou suppliest all I need of food and drink,†
And thou keepest watch over my mouth when I speak.
Ah, may Thōth succour me to-morrow!
Come to me, when I enter the presence of the Lords of Right,‡
And (so will I) go out justified.

---

* The modern Eshmunēn, the great Upper Egyptian centre of the worship of Thōth. The language is probably metaphorical.

† Lit., *bread and beer.*

‡ *I.e.*, the divinities composing the posthumous tribunal.

Thou great dōm-palm, six ells in height!
Thou on whom are fruits!
Stones are in the fruits,
And water is in the stones.

Thou who bringest water to a place afar off,
Come, deliver me, the silent one!

Thōth, the sweet well for one who thirsteth in the wilderness!
It is closed for him who finds words to say.
It is open for the silent.
The silent cometh and findeth the well.*
The hot-headed cometh—but thou art choked.

The idea that man is in closer communion with God and more acceptable to him when he is silent, is also to be found in the writings of the Sage Ani, whose sayings on the subject of duty to parents have been quoted at some length in Chapter I.:

The sanctuary of God, it abhors clamour. Pray with a loving heart, in which all the words remain hidden. Then he doeth what thou requirest; he heareth thy words and accepteth thine offering.

There can be no more suitable ending for this chapter than some extracts from Akhenaton's famous hymn to the sun, of which the king, no doubt justly, claims to be the author, and which so closely resembles the 104th Psalm. In it the sun-

---

* The metaphor is taken from the well in the desert, which is often hidden with pebbles and sand.

god is represented as the All-Father, the source of all life. He it is who has created the different nations and assigned them their divers complexions and languages. He has also provided for their sustenance, making the Nile to well up out of the nether world to water the whole land of Egypt, and setting a Nile in the sky for other peoples, whence it comes down in rain. He is the All-Seeing One and is also seen of all. But to Akhenaton alone has he granted a real measure of understanding of his divine wisdom and power:

Beautiful is thine appearing in the horizon of heaven,
Thou living sun, the first who lived!
Thou risest in the eastern horizon,
Thou fillest every land with thy beauty. . . .

When thou goest down in the western horizon,
The earth is in darkness as if it were dead. . . .
Men sleep in their chambers with head wrapped up,
And none seeth the other. . . .
Every lion cometh forth from his den,
And all snakes that bite.
Darkness (reigns),
The earth is silent,
For he who hath created it rests in his horizon.

When it is dawn and thou risest in the horizon and shinest
  as the sun in the day,
Thou dispellest the darkness and sheddest thy beams.

The Two Lands (Egypt) *keep festival, awake, and stand
    on their feet,
For thou hast raised them up.
They wash their bodies,
They take their clothes,
Their hands (are uplifted) in adoration to thy rising.
The whole land does its work.*

*All cattle are content with their pasture,
The trees and plants flourish.
The birds fly out of their nests,
Their wings (raised) in adoration to thee.
All wild small cattle dance on their feet,
All that fly and flutter—
They live when thou risest for them.*

*The ships voyage down and up stream likewise,
Every way is open, because thou risest.
The fishes in the river leap up before thy face;
Thy rays are in the great green sea. . . .*

*The chick in the egg (already) chirpeth in the shell,
(For) thou givest him breath within it to sustain his life.
Thou makest for him his strength (?) in the egg in order to
    break it;
He cometh forth from the egg to chirp with all his might (?)
He walketh upon his feet when he cometh forth therefrom.*

*How manifold are thy works,
They are hidden from me,
O sole god, to whom none is to be likened. . . .*

The lands of Syria and Ethiopia,
The land of Egypt,
Every man thou settest in his place,
Thou suppliest their needs.
Everyone possesseth his sustenance,
And the length of his days is reckoned.
Their tongues are separate in speech,
And their character likewise.
Their skin is different,
(For) thou distinguishest between the peoples.

Thou makest the Nile in the underworld,
Thou bringest it (up) as thou desirest,
In order to sustain the life of the people of Egypt. . . .

All distant strange lands,
Thou makest their sustenance.
Thou puttest for them a Nile in the firmament.
It comes down for them,
It makes wells upon the hills like the great green sea,
In order to water their fields in their townships.

How excellent are thy designs, O Lord of Eternity!
The Nile in the firmament, thou givest it to the strange peoples,
And to all the wild beasts of the wilderness who go upon their feet.
(But) the (real) Nile it wells up from the nether world for Timuris. . . .

Thou didst make the sky afar in order to rise therein,
In order to behold all that thou hast made . . .
Cities, townships, fields, road and river—

*All men behold thee over against them,
For thou art Aton of the day aloft.* . . .

*Thou art in my heart,
There is none other that knoweth thee,
Save thy son Neferkheprurē ͑ Wa ͑-nerē ͑ (Akhenaton),
Thou makest him to comprehend thy designs and thy
power.* . . .

CHAPTER VII

SOME FUNERARY TEMPLES

THE city of Thebes was divided by the Nile into two parts, a western and an eastern. The eastern half was the main city, containing the residential and business quarters and the great temples of Luxor and Karnak. The western half, to which was attached the vast Theban necropolis, seems to have been largely occupied by the officials, great and small, who had charge of the necropolis, and by the host of artisans subordinate to them, whose business it was to excavate and decorate the tombs and tomb-chapels and keep them in repair, and to manufacture and supply the elaborate funerary equipment, with which every upper and middle-class Egyptian of the Imperial Age wished to be furnished at death. Here also were the workshops of the embalmers and their residences.

At the foot of the hills and towering cliffs, which form the background of the Theban plain on the western side of the river, extends a long

COLOSSAL STATUE, THEBES.
One of a pair placed at the entrance of the funerary temple of Amenhotpe III.
(See p. 188.)

SOME FUNERARY TEMPLES 161

line of temples — the funerary temples of the great emperors of the Eighteenth, Nineteenth, and Twentieth Dynasties. These splendid buildings, however, were not only intended to provide for the posthumous welfare of the Pharaohs who erected them, but they were also dedicated to the worship of the State-god, Amūn. Apart from the actual temple buildings, the sacred precincts included gardens and orchards, ornamental lakes, storehouses, cattle-sheds, the dwellings of the priests, and the quarters of the numberless slaves, mostly foreign captives, who worked on the temple estates as agricultural labourers or herdsmen, or as masons, joiners, and the like. As we shall see, to one temple at least a school was attached, just as schools are often associated with mosques at the present day.

Several of the great Pharaohs, Hatshepsut, Amenḥotpe III., Ramesses II., and Ramesses III., are known to have built themselves palaces adjoining, or in close proximity to, their funerary temples. In the ruins of Amenḥotpe's palace was found the beautiful fragment of ceiling decoration figured and discussed on pp. 80 foll.

In the space of one chapter it is impossible to describe all the magnificent remains of western

Thebes in any detail. It will be best, therefore, to devote the following pages to the discussion of points not usually brought forward in the guide books or in popular works dealing with Ancient Egypt.

The most famous, and probably the most beautiful, of all the royal funerary temples is that of Queen Ḥatshepsut, which, like all the others, was dedicated to the worship of Amūn, but also contained chapels of Anubis, the tutelary god of the dead, and the goddess Ḥathor, in whose cult women figured so prominently. This temple with its three terraces, each connected with the other by an inclined way, and its beautiful colonnades composed of rectangular and polygonal columns, is a unique product of Egyptian architectural genius. It has already been mentioned above how the great queen placed the incense-trees she had brought from Punt along the terraces, in imitation of the tree-clad slopes of Somaliland. A drawing of the temple as it appears at the present day is to be seen on Plate XV.

In the southern half of the colonnade, at the back of the second or middle terrace, are the reliefs depicting Ḥatshepsut's expedition to Punt. The northern half (see Plate XVI.) contains the representations of her divine birth, her reception by the sun-god at Heliopolis, her presentation to the notables of Egypt by her father, and her coronation, of which events the last three have been described at some length in Chapter V.

The reliefs and accompanying inscriptions relating to the queen's birth have already been referred to in Chapter III., where mention was made of a similar series of scenes in the temple of Luxor. They are of first-rate interest and importance, and well deserve our notice.

In the first scene we see Amūn addressing the nine great divinities, the ennead, of Heliopolis, and informing them of his intention to beget a new ruler of Egypt, to whom he promises every blessing.

In the next scene Amūn is shown speaking to Thōth, whom he questions about Aḥmōse, the mother that is to be of Ḥatshepsut. Thōth replies that Aḥmōse is more *beautiful than all women*, and he is depicted in the next relief leading Amūn to her. The text accompanying this latter scene is that rendered above on pp. 68 foll., which relates how Amūn *made his mode of being the majesty* of the reigning Pharaoh, and how he came by night into the sleeping queen's chamber.

We next see the god and Aḥmōse seated side by side and conversing with one another (Fig. 37). The queen says to Amūn: *My lord, how great is thy glory! Splendid is it to behold thy presence. Thou hast filled my majesty with thine excellence. Thy dew is in all my limbs.*

Fig. 37.—Amūn and the Mother of the Prospective Pharaoh. (*After* Gayet, "*Temple de Louxor.*")

Amūn on his part tells the queen that Ḥatshepsut is to be *the name of this thy son** *whom I have planted in thy womb*, and he forecasts for the child a glorious and happy reign. This, like all the other scenes of the series in question, is depicted in a symbolical manner. Amūn appears in his divine form, not in the guise of the queen's husband, and, in order to indicate the ecstatic and heavenly nature of the visitation, the pair are

---

* The masculine word shows that the text is traditional, and referred to all the Pharaohs, and was not specially composed for Ḥatshepsut.

SOME FUNERARY TEMPLES 165

represented as seated upon the sign for heaven, which is raised aloft by two goddesses high above the bed on which the queen had been lying.

In subsequent scenes we see Amūn bidding the potter-god, Khnūm, fashion the body of the promised child; Khnūm actually engaged in modelling the child and its *ka*, or double, on his wheel, while Ḥeḳet, his consort, extends the symbol of life to the child's face (see Fig. 38); and Thōth announcing to Queen Aḥmōse that she will give birth to an heiress and daughter of Geb.*

Fig. 38.—Khnūm fashioning the Unborn Child.

(*After Gayet.*)

Next come representations of the royal accouchement and incidents connected therewith. Khnūm and Ḥeḳet (in the Luxor reliefs Ḥathor takes the place of Ḥeḳet) lead the pregnant queen to the

* The earth-god and a primæval king of Egypt, in which capacity he was, like Rēʻ, a divine pattern of kingship.

place where she is to be delivered, the god assuring her that *she who opens thy womb shall be greater than all (other) kings.*

During the actual birth, which takes place in the presence of Amūn and other divinities, the queen sits on her couch, and four goddesses, presided over

Fig. 39.—Birth of the Sun-God's Human Heir.
(*After Gayet.*)

by Meskhent, the goddess of birth, offer her their assistance in the capacity of midwives (Fig. 39). In addition to the greater divinities already enumerated, a number of genii, including the "souls" of the pre-dynastic kings of Upper and Lower Egypt (see p. 117), are depicted kneeling in two rows and offering the queen the symbol of life. In the middle of these two rows are the symbols of

SOME FUNERARY TEMPLES 167

protection, good fortune, life, stability, and millions of years,* and in the lower row, at the foot of the bed, the figures of the grotesque demi-god Bes† and the hippopotamus-goddess Tawēret.‡ These symbols and figures really constituted the decora-

Fig. 40.—Hathor presenting the New-Born Child to Amūn.
(*After Gayet.*)

tion of the bed, appearing regularly as carvings on the foot-boards of extant couches and on the sides and backs of chairs. The way in which the last-mentioned divinities are here depicted admirably

* In the Luxor relief here reproduced the sign for stability is omitted.
† Generally depicted as a dancer wearing a lion-mask.
‡ The goddess of the *enceinte*.

illustrates the Egyptian idea with regard to the purpose of such decoration—it ensured the actual presence of the beings represented, who would extend their protection to those who reclined or sat on the couch or chair.

The queen safely delivered, the goddess Hathor presents the child to Amūn, *whose heart is very happy* (see Fig. 40). After dandling her on his knee and kissing her, the god appoints divine nurses to suckle the child and its *ka*, among them being the tutelary goddesses of Upper and Lower Egypt, the scorpion goddess Selket, and the sacred *Hesat*-cow identified with both Isis and Hathor. In the adjacent cut (Fig. 41) the queen is seen sitting on her bed with a goddess supporting her, while in front of her two divinities (cow-headed in the Deir el-Baḥri version of the scene) are actively engaged in the duty assigned to them. Below the couch again two sacred cows perform the same office as the two last-mentioned divinities.

Of the four final reliefs, the two most interesting represent the gods determining the duration of the new-born infant's life,—their decision being entered in a book by Seshat, the goddess of reckoning—and Anubis rolling a sieve in front of him. This last-mentioned practice in connection with the

TOMBS OF THE KINGS.
View towards upper end of valley.

birth of a child is still found surviving in the oases of Khargeh and Dakhleh. It is the custom in these localities to place a child seven days after its birth in a sieve along with some salt and grains of

Fig. 41.—The Suckling of the Child.
(*After Gayet.*)

corn, which are sifted through and scattered in the village. " The ceremony is then completed by the father of the child trundling the sieve like a hoop through the streets of the village. . . . The sieve is trundled about so that when the child grows up he may be able to run quickly."*

The next funerary temple that must engage our attention here is that of Ramesses II., commonly called the Ramesseum, of which unfortunately only about half survives.

The inner face of the great towered gateway or pylon—the outer face is just a jumble of fallen stones—is covered with reliefs illustrating or relating to Ramesses' war with the Hittites. On the northern tower the enemy chariotry are breaking into the Egyptian camp; on the southern tower Ramesses, single-handed, drives the routed foe before him into the river Orontes, the feat immortalized in the poem quoted above on pp. 141-144.

Of the outer court, lying behind the pylon, and once colonnaded, only fragments of the west wall remain, in front of which, broken in pieces, lies a gigantic granite statue of Ramesses. When complete and erect it stood nearly sixty feet high and weighed about a thousand tons (see Plate XVII.)!

The second court, which is somewhat better preserved, was colonnaded on all four sides. On the north and south sides were two rows of papyrus-bud columns, while on the east and west

* "Ancient Egypt," 1915, p. 88.

SOME FUNERARY TEMPLES 171

sides was a single row of rectangular pillars with so-called Osirid statues of the Pharaoh in front, and, on the west side of the court only, behind the pillars a corresponding number of columns like those above mentioned. Some of the columns in the northern half of the court are still standing, as

Fig. 42.—The Battle of Kadesh.
(*After* Breasted.)

are also some of the pillars decorated with the Osirid statues, all the statues except one, however, being now headless (see Plates XVIII. and XX.).

On the lower part of the northern half of the east wall of this court is yet another representation of Ramesses' great achievement at the battle of Kadesh. The adjoining cut (Fig. 42) is a drawing of the northern portion of the relief, wherein the Pharaoh is seen charging the fleeing and prostrate foe. Fig. 36 on p. 145, which shows the king of Aleppo being held upside down by his soldiers, and fugitives swimming across the river and being pulled out by their friends on the other side, is a drawing of part of the southern half of the same relief. Close to the group of figures engaged in resuscitating the king of Aleppo stood the Hittite monarch in his chariot—the relief is badly damaged just here—with eight thousand footguards drawn up beside him. Above them is depicted the walled city of Kadesh, surrounded by two moats (see Fig. 43).

The upper portion of the same half of the wall is devoted to a representation of the great annual harvest festival, about which more will be said in connection with a similar relief in the funerary temple of Ramesses III. (see below, pp. 179 foll.).

Three stairways led up to the western colonnade, which was raised on a sort of terrace. On either side of the central flight of steps was a colossal statue of the king in red granite, fragments of which still strew the ground. Three doors in the wall at the back of this colonnade admit to a great hypostyle hall, the roof of which was borne on

SOME FUNERARY TEMPLES 173

forty-eight columns. The nave, consisting of three aisles, is higher than the side-aisles, and the space

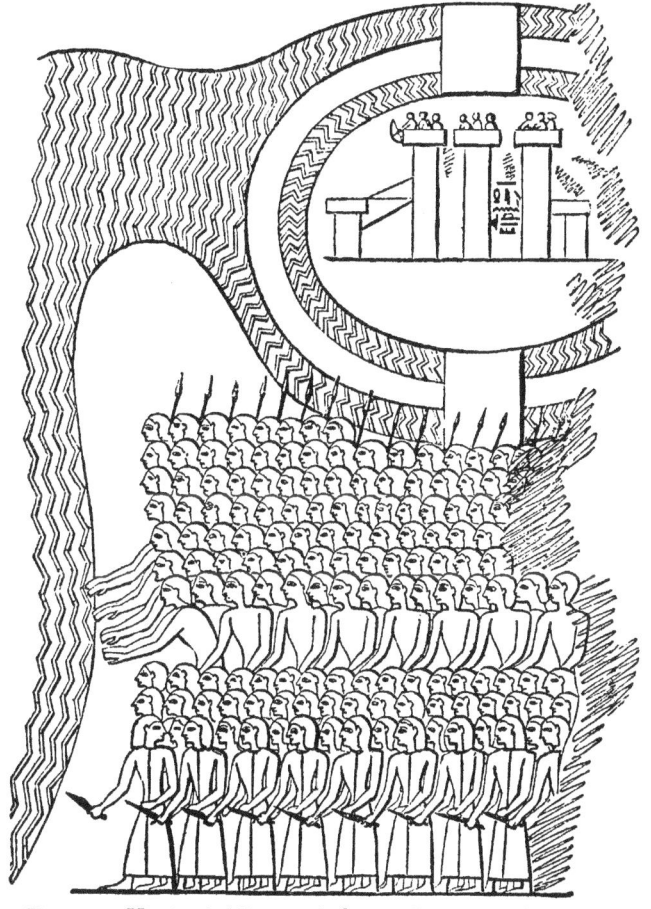

Fig. 43.—Hittite Soldiers and the Walled City of Kadesh.
(*After Baikie, " The Story of the Pharaohs "*)

between the two roof levels is occupied by grated clerestory windows. Many of the columns in the

174 LUXOR AND ITS TEMPLES

side aisles have disappeared, together with most of the once gorgeous colouring; but, despite its ruinous condition, the hall is still most impressive, as can be plainly seen from the drawings on Plates XVII. and XIX.

On the southern half of the east wall of this hall

Fig. 44.—The Attack on Dapur.
(*After Lepsius.*)

is a well-preserved relief depicting the storming of the Hittite fortress of Dapur (see **Fig. 44**). Ramesses II. in his chariot dashes in among the flying enemy who flee towards the city, against the walls of which the Egyptian troops are already placing their scaling-ladders. Some of the fugitive Hittites, it will be noted, are being hauled up into the city by means of ropes, the gates having been

SOME FUNERARY TEMPLES 175

shut upon them. A similar incident occurred, it will be remembered, after Dhutmōse's defeat of the Syrians outside Megiddo (see above, p. 95).

Behind this large hall are two much smaller halls. The first of these has a ceiling decorated with interesting astronomical representations; the second is half destroyed. The sanctuary and its surrounding chambers, as also yet another columned hall, have been completely destroyed.

Some of the ruined brick buildings, which still surround the temple on three sides, were evidently magazines and offices, others being possibly the dwellings of the priests. Included among them was a school, the proof of the existence of which lies in the fact that a number of flakes of limestone covered with writing in ink — ostraca is the technical term—have been found scattered about the ruins, and especially in a small rubbish mound. These ostraca were the "slates" of the Ancient Egyptian schoolboys, who, when they had shown up their writing exercises and had had them duly corrected, threw them away, just as we should throw away used-up sheets of foolscap. On these ostraca are found choice passages from well-known literary works, which the boys were made to write out, perhaps at dictation, both in order to teach them the very difficult and complicated Egyptian script, and also to familiarize them with the literary language and so give them some idea of style.

Evidently the schoolboys of the second millennium B.C. were just as stupid and neglectful as those of to-day. The following admonitions, among many others of a similar character, were regularly given to the Theban boy to write out by way of an exercise in calligraphy, and also, no doubt, to improve his mind: *O writer, be not idle, be not idle, lest thou be soundly chastised. Set not thine heart on pleasures or thou wilt come to destruction. Write with thine hand, read with thy mouth, and ask counsel of those who know more than thou. . . . Pass not a day in idleness, or thou wilt be beaten. The ear of a boy is in his back, he listens when he is beaten. . . . Write on, sicken not of it. Be attentive, hearken to my words. Thou wilt find them profitable.* Such excellent sentiments are not surpassed in modern copy-books!

The best preserved of all the mortuary temples, with the exception perhaps of Hatshepsut's at Deir el-Bahri, is that of Ramesses III., the largest of the group of three temples at Medīnet Habu, of which the other two date, the one from the Eighteenth

SOME FUNERARY TEMPLES

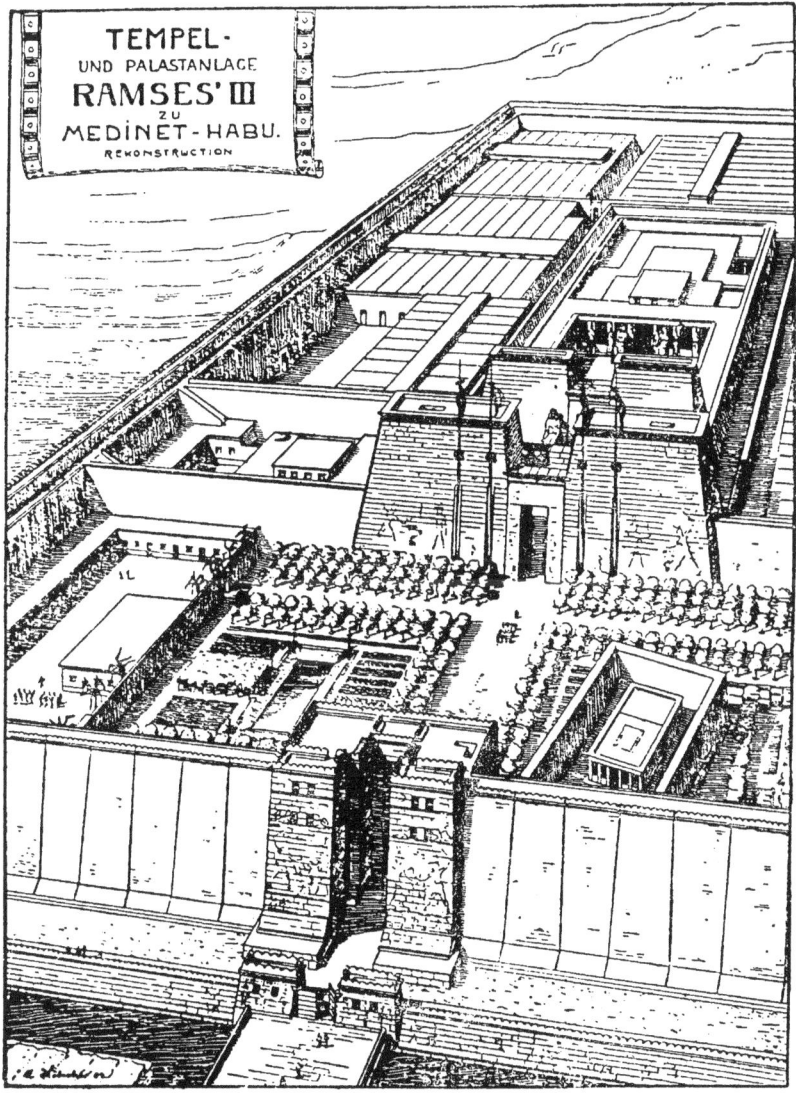

Fig. 45.—The Temple of Medīnet Habu.
(*After* Hölscher, "*Das hohe Tor von Medinet-Habu.*")

Dynasty,* and the other from the Saite Period (see Plate I.). Ramesses surrounded his temple with crenellated walls eighteen metres high and over seven metres thick, the total area enclosed measuring two hundred and ten by three hundred and thirty-five metres; within the walls was included the above-mentioned Eighteenth Dynasty temple. Fig. 45, a restoration by the German archæologist Hölscher, shows what the temple and its surroundings appeared like when intact.

We will first confine our attention to the main temple buildings, which closely resemble in plan the Ramesseum. A pylon admits to a court with a colonnade on the north and south sides, that on the south forming the façade of Ramesses' palace, which was built along this side of the temple. Three doors in the wall behind the southern colonnade admitted to the palace, and in the centre is a large balcony window, where the Pharaoh would show himself to his subjects on special occasions (*cf.* above, p. 103). Ramesses tells us that this palace was *like the great house of Atum* (the sun-god) *which is in heaven. The columns, door-posts, and doors were of gold* (*i.e.*, overlaid with gold). *The great balcony window for the appearance* (of the king) *was*

* Restored and enlarged by the Ethiopian and Saite Pharaohs and by the Ptolemies.

SOME FUNERARY TEMPLES 179

of gold—that is to say, the decorations around the window were overlaid or encrusted with the precious metal. A second pylon at the back (west side) of the court admits to another court, which is colonnaded on all four sides (Plate XXI.). The great hall of twenty-four columns, the cultus-chambers on the north, and the store-chambers on the south side of it, as well as the rooms behind it—namely, two smaller hypostyle halls, the sanctuary and its associated chambers—are now all roofless and in a very ruinous condition.

The inner face of the first pylon is decorated with reliefs illustrating the war which Ramesses III. waged with the Libyans in the eleventh year of his reign, and which has been discussed above in Chapter IV., pp. 108 foll. On the outer face of the second pylon are reliefs and inscriptions referring to his victorious campaign in Syria against the league of northern nations (see above, pp. 104 foll.).

The upper part of the walls behind the colonnades in the northern half of the second court are devoted to a representation of the great harvest festival, yearly celebrated in honour of Min and apparently also in commemoration of the Pharaoh's accession.

In the first scene (Fig. 46) we see the Pharaoh carried in procession from his palace to the temple of Min. He is seated in a canopied litter, elaborately decorated, which is borne on the shoulders of twelve of his sons. Flabellifers walk in front of, behind, and beside him. Behind the litter and its bearers walk courtiers, high officials, and soldiers, and in front of it three priests, two of whom burn incense and the third recites from a book. They

Fig. 46.—The Pharaoh carried in State to the Temple of Min.
(*After Wilkinson.*)

are preceded by more courtiers and officials, the whole procession being headed by a trumpeter and a drummer, and men rattling castanets.

Having arrived at the temple of Min, a fertility god and originally the local divinity of the not far distant city of Coptos, the king made offering to him. This done, the image of Min was placed on a litter draped with a large cloth or carpet which almost swept the ground, and carried in procession by a number of priests, while other priests walked alongside of and behind the image carrying flabellæ, emblems, and shrines (Fig. 47). Immediately in front of the litter marched the Pharaoh, preceded by a white bull (the sacred animal of Min), the queen, an officiant reciting from a book, and a long

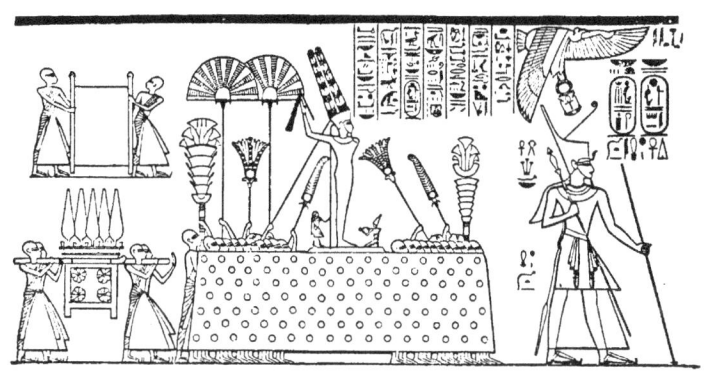

Fig. 47.—The Image of Min carried on a Litter.
(*After Wilkinson*)

line of priests carrying standards, cultus-vessels, and statues of the king and his ancestors.

The procession having reached the scene of operations, the so-called "terrace" of the Temple of Min, priests let fly four birds to announce to the four quarters of heaven that *Horus son of Isis and Osiris has assumed the great crown of Upper and Lower Egypt; the king Ramesses III. has assumed the great crown of Upper and Lower Egypt* (see

Fig. 48). The Pharaoh is next shown (Fig. 49) holding a sickle in his hand and making offering first of a newly reaped sheaf of spelt and then of one of barley; a priest stands ready to take either sheaf from the royal hand. At this performance the king, in his capacity of Horus, is said to be *reaping barley for*

Fig. 48.—The Birds flying to the Four Quarters of Heaven.
(*After Wilkinson.*)

his father—*i.e.*, for Osiris—thereby, as Dr. A. H. Gardiner points out, vindicating his title to the kingship and his patrimony as son of Osiris.* While the Pharaoh was thus engaged a lector recited formulæ from a book, and the queen also sang or

* A. H. Gardiner, "Journal of Egyptian Archæology," ii., p. 125.

SOME FUNERARY TEMPLES 183

repeated some hymn or spell, whereby she is said to *make the king triumph over his enemies.*

The outside of the temple walls, be it here noted, are covered with most interesting historical reliefs, commemorating for the most part the wars of

Fig. 49.—The Pharaoh offering a Sheaf of Barley.
(*After Wilkinson.*)

Ramesses III. Thus the naval battle, figured on p. 107, is on the outside north wall of the second court.

Perhaps the most interesting building at Medînet Habu is the so-called High Gate, which, instead of the usual pylon, forms the entrance to the temple precincts. The walls of the two towers composing the gate are almost straight, and have not that batter which is such a distinctive feature of the walls of the ordinary pylon. The space between the towers gets narrower and narrower as one passes inwards, and finally, as can be seen in Fig. 45, and Plate XXII., they are united by a third tower, in the middle of which is the gateway.

The towers consisted of a ground floor and two upper stories, the latter lit by windows, once filled with wooden gratings and commanding a wonderful view of the Nile Valley. In the foreground lay the tree-encircled lake (see below, p. 187) and the wide expanse of fertile fields stretching endlessly north and south; in the near distance the glimmering waters of the great river, and eastern Thebes with its gorgeous temples; and behind all these the precipitous hills of the Red Sea desert, pale and wan-looking in broad daylight, but glowing like amethysts in the rays of the setting sun.

Just below the first-story windows on the inner face of the two flanking towers are curious brackets decorated with the heads and shoulders of foreign captives, and on them once stood statues of Ramesses smiting his enemies.

SOME FUNERARY TEMPLES 185

These upstairs apartments were evidently assigned to the royal ḥarīm, when the court was in residence in the palace adjoining the temple, as is suggested by the reliefs decorating their walls, these representing the king surrounded by his women. A typical example of them is Fig. 50, which shows his majesty playing draughts with one of his ḥarīm-favourites, who holds out a posy for her lord to smell.

The High Gate is almost certainly non-Egyptian in its general design, and the usually accepted view is that it was copied from the towered gates admitting to the Syrian or Babylonian fenced cities.

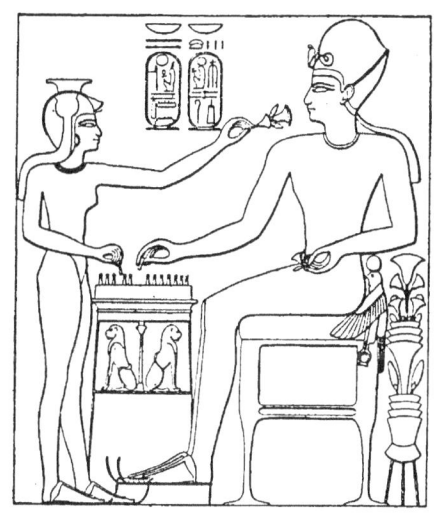

Fig. 50.—Ramesses III. with One of the Ladies of his Ḥarīm.

(*After* Wilkinson.)

The temple of Ramesses III. was most magnificent, both in its decoration and in its furnishing, and, like all the royal funerary temples, was richly endowed. The reliefs and inscriptions inside and outside the building were brilliantly coloured. *The doors, we are told, were of gold and copper in beaten work. Its towers were of stone soaring heavenwards, adorned and carved with the chisel. The cultus-image of Amūn was adorned with real costly stones like the horizon, and when it appeared in processions men rejoiced to behold it.* Many of the vessels employed in the service of the god were *of fine gold*, and there were *others of silver and copper without number*. The temple treasury, still perfectly preserved, was filled with *gold, silver, and every costly stone by the hundred thousand*.

The temple had its own flotilla of ships on the river, and these came *laden with barley and wheat for transport without cessation to its granary*, which consequently was always *overflowing with* grain. As for *the fields* belonging to the temple *and its herds, their multitudes were like the sand of the shore*.

The funerary temple of Amenhotpe III. was similarly endowed and equipped. *Its barns*, the Pharaoh asserts, *contain good things without number. . . . Its cattle are like the sand of the shore, they make up millions. . . . Its storehouse is filled with male and female servants, with the children of the princes of all foreign countries which his majesty has captured. . . . It* (the temple) *is surrounded with*

SOME FUNERARY TEMPLES 187

settlements of Syrians, colonized with the children of princes.

Not far from the walled-in precincts of his temple, in order to secure to it a constant supply of water, Ramesses III. excavated a great lake, which was *planted with trees and vegetation like the Delta.* Within the precincts *were gardens and places with arbours, filled with fruits and flowers.* There was also *a pool, supplied with lotus flowers* (see Fig. 45). Such a pool seems to have been as essential an adjunct to a funerary temple as to one entirely dedicated to the worship of the gods. Thus the precincts of Amenhotpe III.'s funerary temple contained *a pool full (of water), like a high Nile, the lord of fish and fowl.*

The description bequeathed us by Ramesses III. of his great temple at Medīnet Habu gives us some idea of the almost overpowering magnificence of the public buildings of western Thebes, a magnificence which had, however, reached its culmination some two centuries earlier in the already twice mentioned funerary temple of Amenhotpe III., utterly destroyed, alas! by that vandal Merneptah in his search for a plentiful and cheap supply of building material wherewith to erect his own funerary temple. An avenue lined with statues of jackals—

the tutelary divinity of the necropolis was the jackal-god Anubis—led from the river bank to the vast pylon admitting to the colonnaded forecourt. The pylon, the towers of which were furnished with the usual flag-staffs *wrought with gold*, bore the name *Amūn-has-received-his-sacred-barque* (i.e., boat - shrine); for, besides serving as the main entrance to the temple, the pylon was intended to be used as a halting-place or station for the processional image of Amunrēʻ, when, on the occasion of the yearly funerary festival called the *Festival of the Valley*, that god was conveyed across the river to visit *the divinities of the West* —i.e., of the necropolis.

Two colossal portrait-statues of Amenḥotpe, either seventy feet high and fashioned out of a single block of sandstone, were set up before the pylon, and with them also a pair of obelisks. The two statues are the well-known colossi of Memnon (see Plate XXIII.), the northern one being the famous "Vocal Memnon." According to certain of the Classical writers, this statue emitted a musical note at the time of sunrise, a phenomenon first recorded by the geographer Strabo (who flourished about 20 B.C.) and only noticed, by the way, after the upper portion had been shattered and split off by an earthquake in the early days of the Roman Empire. When the statue had been piously, though somewhat crudely, restored by Septimius Severus, it ceased to be "vocal" altogether. These two mutilated statues are practically all that remains of the once glorious building, which, in the words of the Pharaoh himself, *was an eternal everlasting fortress of good white sandstone wrought with gold throughout. Its floor*, he goes on to say, *is overlaid with silver, and all its gates with gold. It abounds in statues of the king made of granite from Aswān, of wonderful stones, and all kinds of splendid costly stones.* These particular statues, it would seem, were those set up in the colonnades of the forecourt.

The place where the king stood, when he pontificated at the celebration of the liturgy, was marked by a great sandstone stela, thirty feet high and inlaid with gold and costly stones, which now lies prostrate and broken behind the colossi. No wonder that it was said of the whole glittering edifice that *it resembles the horizon of heaven with Rē rising therein.*

BIBLIOGRAPHY

Baedecker, K. : *Egypt and the Sûdân*, 1914, pp. 253-332.

Benson, M., and J. Gourlay : *The Temple of Mut in Asher*. London, 1899.

Birch, S. : *Facsimile of an Egyptian Hieratic Papyrus of the Reign of Ramses III., now in the British Museum*. London, 1876; pls. iv., lines 1-4, 6, 7, 11, 12 ; v., lines 1-3.

Blackman, A. M. : *A New Chapter in the History of Egyptian Art* in *Discovery*, iii., pp. 35-40.

Libations to the Dead in Modern Nubia and Ancient Egypt, in *The Journal of Egyptian Archæology*, iii., pp. 31-34.

The Position of Women in the Ancient Egyptian Hierarchy, op. cit., vii., pp. 8-30.

Priest, Priesthood (Egyptian); Purification (Egyptian); Worship (Egyptian), in Hastings, *Encyclopædia of Religion and Ethics*.

The Rock Tombs of Meir, i.-iii. London, 1914-15.

The Sun-Cult in Ancient Egypt, in *Nature*, April 14 and 21, 1923.

Borchardt, L. : *Voruntersuchung von Tell el-Amarna in Januar*, 1907, in *Mitteilungen der deutschen Orient-Gesellschaft*, No. 34, pp. 20-28.

Ausgrabungen in Tell el-Amarna 1911, op. cit., No. 46, pp. 14-25.

Ausgrabungen in Tell el-Amarna 1911-12, op. cit., No. 50, pp. 9-22.

Ausgrabungen in Tell el-Amarna 1912-13, op. cit., No. 52, pp. 10-23.

Breasted, J. H. : *A History of Egypt*. London, 1906 ; pp. 111-501.

Ancient Records. Chicago, 1906 ; i., §§ 391-414, 640-748; ii., §§ 1-37, 67-80, 221-242, 246-295, 391-443, 450-451, 783, 785-797, 883-889, 917; iv., §§ 35-113, 189, 190, 192, 193, 416-456.

The Cambridge Ancient History. Cambridge, 1923; i., pp. 284-315.

Daressy, G. : *La Grande Colonnade du Temple de Louxor*, in *Mémoires publiés par les Membres de la Mission archéologique française au Caire*; viii., pt. 3. Cairo, 1894 ; pls. i.-xvi., pp. 380-391.

Notice explicative des ruines de temple de Louxor. Cairo, 1893.

Notice explicative des ruines du temple de Médinet Habou. Cairo, 1897.

BIBLIOGRAPHY

Davies, N. de G. : *The Rock Tombs of El-Amarna*. London, 1903-1908; vi., pl. xxvii., pp. 29-31.
The Tomb of Nakht at Thebes. New York, 1917 ; pls. x., xv.-xvii., xxii.-xxiv., pp. 55-59, 66-69.
The Tomb of Puyemrê at Thebes. New York, 1922 ; i., pls. vii.-xi., xli., xlii., pp. 45-57.

Duemichen, J. : *Altägyptische Tempelinschriften*. Leipzig, 1867 ; ii., pl. xxxviii., lines 16-19.
Historische Inschriften. Leipzig, 1867-1869 ; i., pls. xv., xvi., lines 25-34, xx., line 3 ; ii., pl. xlvi., lines 22-24.
Egyptian Hieratic Papyri in the British Museum. London, 1923; ii., pls. xli.-xliv.

Erman, A. : *Aegypten und aegyptisches Leben im Altertum*, neu bearbeitet von Hermann Ranke. Tübingen, 1923 ; pp. 175-230, 263-293.
Die Literatur der Aegypter. Leipzig, 1923 ; pp. 109-119, 130-148, 197-216, 243-245, 296, 299, 305, 307, 309, 311-313, 315, 320-322, 325-335, 346-348, 355, 358-362, 377, 378, 380-383.
Der syrische Feldzug Amenophis II., in *Zeitschrift für ägyptische Sprache*, xxvii., pp. 39-41.
Zur ägyptischen Religion, op. cit., xlii., pp. 106-109.

Gardiner, A. H., and N. de G. Davies : *The Tomb of Amenemhēt*. London, 1915 ; pls. i.-ix., xv., xvi., xviii., xxi., pp. 26-67.

Gardiner, A. H. : *New Literary Works from Ancient Egypt*, in *The Journal of Egyptian Archæology*, i., pp. 20-36, 100-106.
The Defeat of the Hyksos by Kamōse : "The Carnarvon Tablet, No. I.," op. cit., iii., pp. 95-110.
The Delta Residence of the Ramessides, op. cit., v., pp. 127-138, 179-200, 242-271.

Gauthier, H. : *Le Temple d'Amada*. Cairo, 1913 ; pp. 22, 23, lines 16-23.

Gayet, A. : *Le Temple de Louxor*. Cairo, 1894 ; pls. lxiii.-lxvii.

Golénischeff, W. : *Les Papyrus hiératiques, Nos. 1115, 1116A, and 1116B de l'Ermitage impérial de St. Petersbourg*, 1913, pls. ix.-xiv., xxiii.-xxv.

Grébaut, E. : *Hymne à Ammon-Ra des Papyrus égyptiens du Musée de Boulaq*. Paris, 1874.

Greene, J. B. : *Fouilles exécutees à Thebès dans l'année 1855*. Paris, 1855 ; pl. ii., lines 20-24.

Griffith, F. L. : *The Inscriptions of Siût and Dêr Rîfeh*. London, 1891 ; pls. 11-15, 20.

Gunn, B., and A H. Gardiner : *New Renderings of Egyptian Texts : II. The Expulsion of the Hyksos*, in *The Journal of Egyptian Archæology*, v., pp. 36-56.

Hölscher, U. : *Das hohe Tor von Medinet Habu*. Leipzig, 1910.

BIBLIOGRAPHY

Legrain, G. : *Louqsor sans les Pharaons.* Paris, 1914 ; pp. 47-91.

Lepsius, C. R. : *Denkmäler aus Aegypten und Aethiopien.* Berlin, 1849-59 ; iii., pls. 162-166, 170, 171, 212, 213.

Mackay, E. : *Origin of Polychrome Borders,* in Ancient Egypt, 1916, pp. 169-173.

Mariette, A. : *Karnak.* Leipzig, 1875 ; pls. 28-31.

Maspero, G. : *Art in Egypt.* London, 1912 ; pp. 146, 147.
Popular Stories of Ancient Egypt. London, 1915 ; pp. 269-274.

Meyer, E. : *Geschichte des Altertums.* Stuttgart and Berlin, 1913 ; pp. 188-327.

Möller, G. : *Hieratische Lesestücke für den akademischen Gebrauch.* Leipzig, 1909-1910 ; iii., pls. 13-15.

Müller, W. M. : *Die Liebespoesie der alten Ägypter.* Leipzig, 1899.

Naville, E. : *The Temple of Deir El Bahari.* London, 1895-1908 ; pls. xlvi.-lxxxvi.

Peet, T. E. : *Excavations in Tell El-Amarna,* in The Journal of Egyptian Archæology, vii., pp. 170-178.

Petrie, W. M. F. : *A History of Egypt.* London, 1917-1923 ; i., pp. 79 to end ; ii. ; iii., pp. 1-165.
Egyptian Tales. London, 1895 ; ii., pp. 13-86.
Six Temples at Thebes 1896. London, 1897 ; pls. xi.-xiv.
Tell el Amarna. London, 1894 ; pls. i.-ix.

Rougé, E. de : *Inscriptions hiéroglyphiques.* Paris, 1877 ; pls. cxxv., lines 25-34, cxli., lines 22-24, clxxv.-clxxvi.
Select Papyri in the Hieratic Character from the Collections of the British Museum. London, 1841-1860 ; pls. viii., lines 2-6 ; xxiv.-xxxiv. ; lxx., line 5 to lxxi., line 6 ; lxxvi., line 9, to lxxvii., line 4 ; xcii., line 8, to xciii., line 5.

Sethe, K. : *Urkunden des ägyptischen Altertums.* Leipzig, 1905-1906 ; iv., pp. 3-5, 8, 9, 82-86, 88-90, 245-265, 319-353, 614-618, 647-667, 775-777.
Die Zeitrechnung der alten Aegypten im Verhältniss zu der andern Volker in Nachrichten der K. Gesellschaft der Wissenschaften zu Gottingen. Philologische Klasse, 1919 ; p. 310.

Tylor, J. J., and F. Ll. Griffith : *The Tomb of Paheri at El Kab.* London, 1894 ; pl. vii., pp. 23-25.

Wilkinson, J. G. : *The Manners and Customs of the Ancient Egyptians,* edited by Birch. London, 1878 ; iii., pl. lx. (facing p. 355).

Woolley, C. L. : *Excavations in Tell El-Amarna,* in The Journal of Egyptian Archæology, viii., pp. 49-65.

Wreszinski, W. : *Atlas zur altägyptischen Kulturgeschichte.* Leipzig, pls. 1, 2.

INDEX

'Aamu, 38, 39
Ablutions, 7
Abu 'l-Ḥaggāg, the Sheykh, 78
Abydos, 43, 44
Aḥmōse I., 56, 58, 84, 87, 88, 112
Aḥmōse, Admiral, 88
Aḥmōse, Queen, 112, 163, 164, 165
Akhenaton, 56, 81, 111, 155, 156, 159
Akhthoi, Baron, 45, 46
Akhthoi, King, 43, 45
Aleppo, King of, 144, 145, 172
Amenemḥēt I., 46, 47, 51
Amenemḥēt III., 50, 51
Amenemḥēt IV., 51
Amenḥotpe I., 90
Amenḥotpe II., 98-101
    bow of, 100
Amenḥotpe III, 74
    avenue of sphinxes of, 62
    colonnaded court of (at Luxor), 71
    columned hall of, 64
        unfinished, 65, 67
    funerary temple of, 186, 187
    inscription of, 62
    palace of (at Thebes), 81, 161
    statues of, 62, 188
    temple of (at Luxor), 64
Amenḥotpe IV., 111
Amor, 104, 105
Amūn, 62, 69, 71, 75, 92, 95, 96, 109, 134, 136, 140-142, 163, 164, 166, 168
    as good herdsman, 152
    as protector of poor and defenceless, 153
    as skilful pilot, 153
    as State-god, identified with sun-god Rē'-Atum, 47, 56, 67, 68, 117, 161
    cattle belonging to, 109
    Chief of the Concubines of, 70
    concubines of, 70, 76
    cultus image of, 186
    God's Wife of, 68-70
    prisoners sacrificed to, 100, 104

Amūn, processional image of, 188
    Southern *Harīm* of, 64, 67, 70
    statue (portable) of, 93
    temple of (at Karnak), 62, 64
    temple of (at Pi-Ra'messe), 63
Amunrē', 47, 114, 132
Anarchy, 37
Ani, Sage, 25, 155
Anubis, 162, 168, 188
Anūp, 147
Archers, Asiatic, 52
    Egyptian, 106, 108
'Aruna, 91-94
Asia, 137
Asiatics, 38, 39, 44-46, 51, 54, 84, 86, 94, 98, 99
Askalon, 139
Aswān, 85, 87, 189
Asyūt, 42-46
Athribis, 44
Attendants, female, 4, 17
Atum, 178
Avaris, 54, 55, 85
Avenue (lined with statues of jackals), 187

B

Ba'al, 109, 143
Balcony (of royal palace), 103, 178
Banquets, 22, 28, 30
Bata, 147
Bathroom, 8
Bedrooms, 8
Beehive huts (of Puntites), 132
Beer, 28, 31, 33, 34
Benches (of brick), 4
Benha, 44
Bes, 167
Birds (let fly as carriers of news), 124, 181
Birth, divine (of the Pharaoh), 70, 163
Boat (of papyrus), 13, 15, 16
    (of Sheykh Abu 'l-Ḥaggāg), 78
Boat-shrine, 71, 73, 74-76, 188
Bolshevism, 38
Boxes, 10
Bread and beer, 25, 154

Breasted, Professor, 35, 58, 101, 129, 143
Bureaucratic government, 49
Buto, 75, 117, 122
Byblos, 40

C

Cairo, 4, 44
Calendar, 125
Calligraphy, exercise in, 176
Cambyses, 101
Captives, 100, 103, 108, 109, 141, 161, 186
Carmel, 90, 91
Carnarvon, Lord, 84
  tablet, 84
Carpets, 9
Caskets, 10
Cat, 14
Cataract, first, 87
  fourth, 85
Cattle-sheds, 161
Cedars, 40
Ceiling, painted, 5, 81, 161
Chairs, 9, 28
Chariot, 52, 80, 95, 96, 98, 99, 140, 142, 143
Charioteer, 140, 143, 144
Chariotry, 98, 140, 141
Cilicia, 104
Civil strife, 51
Concubines, 17
Conspiracy, 19, 20
Coptos, 41, 180
Coronation, 120, 121, 146, 163; *cf.* 179
Couches, 10
Cows, sacred, 168
Cowsheds, 4
Crete, 40, 137
Crown, red (of Lower Egypt), 123
  white (of Upper Egypt), 122
Crowns (of Upper and Lower Egypt), 115
Cusæ, 42, 55, 85
Cushions, 10, 82, 137

D

Dais (in reception-room), 6
Dakhleh, oasis of, 169
Dancers, negro, 75
Dancing, 19

Dancing-girls, 31
Dapur, Hittite fortress of, 174
Dau, 27
Daughters, 17
Deir el-Bahri, temple of Hatshepsut at, 70, 113, 115, 117, 121, 128, 135, 162-170
Delta, 39, 42, 44, 45, 51, 54, 79, 83-85, 102, 104, 107, 108, 187
Dendereh, temple of Hathor at, 69
Denyen, 102
Deutsche-Orient-Gesellschaft, 4
Dḥutmōse I., 87-90, 112, 117-119, 125
Dḥutmōse II., 112, 126
Dḥutmōse III., 89-98, 111, 126, 127, 135, 136, 175
  annals of, 89
  festival hall of, 59
Dḥutnūfer, 2
Diadems (of Upper and Lower Egypt), 115, 121; see also under "Crowns"
Dining-room, 6, 8
Division (of Egyptian army), 140
Dōm-palm, 155
Draughts, game of, 185
Drinking, 28
Drummer, 73, 76, 180
  negro, 75
Drunkenness, 32, 77, 79

E

Egypt Exploration Society, 3
Ehnāsīyeh el-Medīneh, 41
Eighteenth Dynasty, 56, 58, 84, 87, 161
Eighth Dynasty, 41
El-Amarna, 4, 5, 56, 81, 82
Elephantine, 85, 141
Eleventh Dynasty, 46, 47
El-Kāb, 88
Enclosure (around house), 4, 5
Erment, 41
Esdraelon, 91
Eshmunēn, 56, 84, 86, 154
Euphrates, 98

F

Fat women, taste for, 130
Father, love of son for, 26, 27
Fayūm, 48
Festival, 76, 77

INDEX 197

Festival, funerary, 188
  of the Valley, 188
Feudal state, 36
  system, 48
Feudatories, 36, 49, 50
Fifth Dynasty, 35
First Dynasty, 122
Fishing, 12
Flabellæ, 181
Flabellifer, 73, 180
Flags (decorating pylon), 66
Flag-staffs, 62, 66, 75, 141, 188
Fleet, Egyptian, 106, 129, 134
Floors, 9
Folk-tales, 147
Fourth Dynasty, 35
Fowling, 12, 14
Frieze, 6
Furnishing, furniture, 9, 80

G

Game, 17
Garden, 10, 12
  botanical and zoological, 60
  (of a temple), 63, 135, 161, 187
Gardiner, Dr A. H., 182
Garland, 30, 34
Gaza, 90
Geb, 165
Geese (as carrier-birds), 124 ; see also under "Birds"
Gezer, 139
God's-Land, 128-133
God's Wife ; see under Amūn
Granaries, 2, 4
Grease, perfumed, 29
Great House, 121
Guests, 29

H

Hamites, 129
Haremheb, 71
Ḥarīm, 19, 20
  royal, 185
  -favourites, 185
Harpoon, 12
Harvest festival, 179
Ḥathor, 68, 69, 162, 168
  temple of (at Dendereh), 69
  (wife of Rē'-Atum), 69, 70
Ḥathors, 77
  the seven, 148

Hatshepsut, 90, 111-135, 146, 161, 163
  funerary temple of (at Deir el-Baḥri), 70, 162-170
Hatsho', 108
Hearth, 8
Heket, 165
Heliopolis, 56, 67, 114, 115, 117, 125, 154
  ennead of, 163
  Hatshepsut's reception by the sun-god at, 163
  temple of Atum at, 69
Herakleopolis, 41, 47, 48
Herakleopolitan art, 42
  supremacy, 41-46
Herakleopolitans, 41
Hermonthis, 142
Hermopolis, 154
Herodotus, 101
Ḥesat-cow, 168
Hierakonpolis, 121
High Gate (at Medinet Habu), 183
High-priestess, queen as, 126
Hippopotamus, 12, 15, 16
Hittite land, 139
Hittite monarch, 172
Hittites, 65, 104, 140, 144, 170
Hólscher, Dr., 178
Horus, 115, 122, 124, 139, 181, 182
Houses, 1, 4
Hunter, 17
Hunting, 12, 17
Husband and wife, relations of, 21-25
Hyksōs, 49, 51, 54, 55, 58, 84-87, 128

I

Image (of a divinity), 71
Incense, 29, 73, 80, 133
  -trees, 133, 162
Intef, 16
Ipet-Isut, 64
Ipuwer, 37-40
Isis, 124, 168, 181
Israel, 139
Ithtōwi, 48, 50

K

Ka, 165
Kadesh, 90, 91, 96-98, 172, 173
  battle of, 171
Kamōse,'55, 56, 84-87

198 INDEX

Karnak, temple of, 58, 60, 62, 63, 70, 71, 76, 160
Keper, 109
Khargeh, oasis of, 169
Khenshotpe, 25
Khnūm, 47, 165
Khons, 71
Kibleh, 6
Kina, 94, 95
Kitchen, 2, 9

L

Ladies, 15
Lake, sacred, 63, 161; see also under "Pool" (excavated by Ramesses III.), 187
Lamps, 30
Lapis-lazuli, 62
Lavatory, 8
Lebanon, 74, 98, 133
Libya, 139
Libyans, 102-104, 107, 138, 179
Lisht, 48
Litter, 179-181
Liturgy, temple, 189
Lotus flowers, 10, 15, 30, 63, 187
Love-songs, 149
Lower Egypt, conquest of, 122
Lustral washing (at coronation), 121
Luxor, temple of, 62, 64, 67, 70, 74, 78, 160, 163

M

Manetho, 51, 54
Masts; see under "Flag-staffs"
Matting, 9
Mayor, 50
Medinet Habu, 105, 106, 176, 183
Megiddo, 91-93, 95-97, 175
Memnon, 188
Memphis, 48, 122
Menes, 122, 123
Menhotpe IV., 46
Menna, 143
Merikerē. 44, 45
Merneptah, 102, 139, 187
Mert-priestesses, 75
Meshersher, 107, 108
Meshwesh, 107-109
Meskhent, 166
Meten, 137

Meyer, Professor Eduard, 51
Middle Kingdom, 136
Min, 179
 image of, 180
 sacred animal of, 181
 temple of, 179-181
Minstrels, 31
Mitanni, 148
Mont, 46, 95, 103, 105, 143
Mosque, 78
Mother, love of son for, 25, 26
Music, 19
Musician-priestesses, 69, 75-77
 -priests, 75
Musicians, 31, 33
Mut, 62, 71
 temple of, 63
Mutnofret, 112

N

Naharin, 91
Napata, 101
Nature (love of Egyptians for), 12
Naval action, 103, 106, 183
Necropolis, Theban, 160
Neferirkerē II., 41
Neferkauhōr, 41
Nefretiri, 67, 112
Nefrusi, 86
Nekhbet, 115, 119, 121
Nekhen, 75, 117
Nesut, 113
Nesut-bīyet, 113
New Year's Day, 70, 120
Nigidius Figulus, 125
Nineteenth Dynasty, 56, 101, 161
Ninth Dynasty, 41
Nitōkris, 112
Nubia, 50, 84, 87, 101, 133
Nubians, 88

O

Obelisks, 65, 75, 83, 141
Officials (salaried), 49
Old Kingdom, 35
Ōpet, festival of, 70. 78
Orchards, 161
Orontes, 98, 102, 144, 170
Osirid statues, 171
Osiris, 124, 154, 181, 182
Ostraca, 175
Ox-carts, 105

INDEX 199

P

Palestine, 90, 98, 136, 139
Papyri (in British Museum), 154
Papyrus Harris, 63
Parks, 12
Pavilion (in garden), 12
Peleset, 101, 102
Pelusium, 54
Perehu, 129
Philistines, 101
Phylæ (of priests), 72
Physician, 24
Piety (to parents), 26, 27
Piles, huts on, 132
Pillar of his Mother, 121
Piōpi I., Piōpi II., 36
Pi-Ra'messe, 54, 56, 63
Poetry, religious, 152
Pond (in garden), 12
Pool (adjunct of temple), 63, 187
Priesthood, 72
Priests (of sun-god), 73
 dwellings of, 161
Prisoners of war, sacrifice of, 104
Procession (at coronation), 122
 (at a festival), 73-76, 179-181
Punt, 128-131, 133, 162
Puntites, 132-135
Purification (at coronation), 122
Pylon, 62, 65, 66, 141

R

Ramesses II., 65, 142, 161
 and Seti I., columned hall of, 60, 62, 65
 (at attack on Dapur), 174
 (at battle of Kadesh), 140-146, 171
 colonnaded court of (at Luxor), 65, 66
 funerary temple of, 170-175
 heroism of, 140
 statues of, 170, 172
Ramesses III., 19, 102-110, 161, 181, 185
 funerary temple of, 172, 176-186
 palace of (at Medīnet Habu), 161, 178
 palace of (at Tell el-Yahūdīyeh), 83
 wars of, 183

Ramesses III., wars of (with Libyans), 102-104, 107-110, 179
 (with northerners), 104-107
Ramesses IV., 146, 147
Ramesseum, 144, 145, 170
Rē', 40, 92, 115, 154
Rē'-Atum, 56, 67, 69, 114, 115, 117
 high-priestess of, 67
Rē'-Ḥarakhte, 147
Reaping (ceremonial), 182
Reception-rooms, 6, 28
Recess (painted), 6
Red Sea, 128, 129
Retenu, 74, 137
Roof (resort of women), 2
Rugs, 9

S

Sacrificing (prisoners of war), 100
Sallier Papyrus No. 1, 154
Scaling ladder, 174
Scent, 29
Scholar, 33
School, 26, 161, 175
Schoolboys, 176
Sea-fight, 107
Sea-rovers, 103, 104, 106
Selket, 168
Sentries, 94
Senzar, 98
Septimius Severus, 189
Servants, 4, 9
 (in a temple), 186, 187
Seshat, 116, 168
Seshed, 137
Sesōstris II., 48
Sesōstris III., 48-51
Sēth, 115, 122, 139, 154
Seti I. and Ramesses II., columned hall of, 60, 62, 65
Seventh Dynasty, 41
Sharuhen, 87
Shat, 138
Shekelesh, 102
Shemesh-Edom, 98
Sherden, 102
Ship (for conveyance of Amūn on ceremonial voyage), 74
Ships, flotilla of (belonging to temple), 186
Shooting, big game, 12
Shrines, 71

Sicilians, 101
Sieve, ceremonial trundling of, 168-170
Sikeloi, 101
"Sisters," 5, 25
Sixth Dynasty, 27, 51, 112
Slaves, 161
Somaliland, 128, 132, 162
Son, 25-27
"Souls" of Buto and Nekhen, 75, 117, 166
Sphinxes, avenue of, 62
Spinning, 2
Stables, 4
Standard-bearers, 122, 124
Standards, 181
Stools, 9
Storehouses, 4, 161
Store-rooms, 9
Strabo, 188
Streets, 1, 34
Sudan, 49
Sudanese, 50, 101
Sun-cult, heliopolitan, 72
Sun-god, 47, 72, 114, 115
 wife of, 68
Syria, 90, 102, 104, 105, 127, 135, 179
Syrians, settlements of (belonging to a temple), 187

T

Tangur, 88
Tawēret, 167
Teacher, 33
Tefibi, 43
Temple, precincts of, 161
Temples, funerary, 161
Tenth Dynasty, 41, 46
Thanēni, 89
Tharu, 90
Thebaid, 41
Thebans, 44, 45, 56
Thebes, 1, 41, 46, 47, 54, 57, 58, 62, 67, 83, 87, 101, 102, 160
Thinite nome, 44

Thōth, 116, 154, 163, 165
 hymn to, 153
Throw-stick, 13, 15
Timuris, 139, 158
To-Nūter, 74, 133, 137
Tombos, 88
Town, Egyptian, 1
Trade, 39, 45
Treasury (of a temple), 187
Trumpeter, 73, 76, 180
Tut'enkhamūn, 71, 149
Twelfth Dynasty, 46, 47, 64, 85
Twentieth Dynasty, 56, 161

U

Uthentyu, 138
Uto, 115, 121

V

Vassals, 36, 37
Vizier, 35

W

Wādy Ṭūmīlāt, 129
Wall-painting, 81
Warships, 105
Washing (before meals), 7, 29
Watches (of priests), 72
Water, holy, 122
 libation of (to the dead), 27
Wax figures (magical), 19
Weaver, weaving, 2
Weld-Blundell, Mr. H., 132
Weshwesh, 102
White Walls (name of Memphis), 123
Wife, 15, 17, 21-25
Wigs, 30
Wine, 28, 31
Women's quarters (in a house), 2, 17
Writing, 26

Y

Yahes, 122
Yehem, 90, 91
Yenoam, 139

www.ingramcontent.com/pod-product-compliance
Lightning Source LLC
Chambersburg PA
CBHW061244230426
43662CB00020B/2419